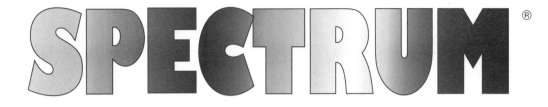

Vocabulary

Grade 5

Published by Spectrum®
an imprint of Carson Dellosa Education
Greensboro, North Carolina

Spectrum®
An imprint of Carson Dellosa Education
P.O. Box 35665
Greensboro, NC 27425 USA

ISBN 978-1-4838-1193-2

05-015247784

Table of Contents

Skills Practice

Test-taking Practice

Name _____

Classification means to put objects together in **groups**.
    Rhinoceros, **human**, and **chimpanzee** are all **mammals**.

Write each animal name in the correct group.

Birds

_____   _____

_____   _____

Amphibians

_____   _____

_____   _____

Reptiles

_____   _____

_____   _____

Fish

_____   _____

_____   _____

Mammals

_____   _____

_____   _____

cobra	aardvark	tuna	rainbow trout	gecko
salmon	killer whale	bullfrog	newt	owl
ostrich	toad	sailfish	salamander	wolf
pelican	bald eagle	Gila monster	chameleon	gorilla

Name _____

THIS CARNIVORE IS QUITE CRANKY!

Circle the word in each group that is unlike the rest.

1. carnivore   herbivore   omnivore   nocturnal

2. quartz   nylon   iron pyrite   turquoise

3. ice   steam   water   pitcher

4. launch pad   comet   planet   asteroid

5. gecko   chameleon   squirrel   Gila monster

6. grasshopper   termite   firefly   anteater

7. circulatory   digestive   metric   nervous

8. pine   sunflower   sunlight   cabbage

9. hurricane   tornado   space   earthquake

10. apple   wheat   soybean   oats

11. whale   shark   tarpon   salmon

12. steel   aluminum   plastic   copper

13. microphone   microscope   telescope   binoculars

An **analogy** uses **word relationships** to compare one group to another group:
Swim is to water as ski is to snow.

Read each sentence carefully. Write the word that completes the sentence on the line.

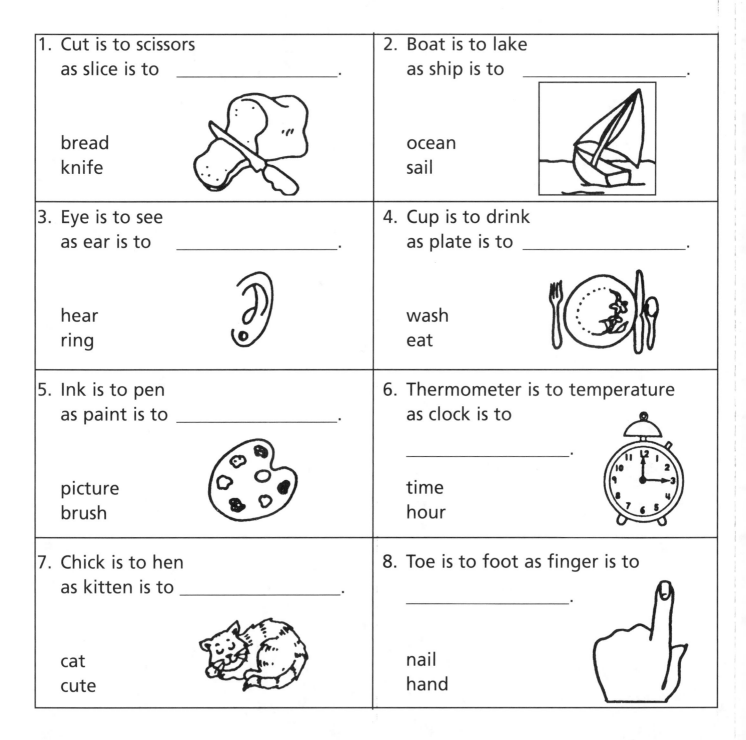

1. Cut is to scissors
   as slice is to _____.

   bread
   knife

2. Boat is to lake
   as ship is to _____.

   ocean
   sail

3. Eye is to see
   as ear is to _____.

   hear
   ring

4. Cup is to drink
   as plate is to _____.

   wash
   eat

5. Ink is to pen
   as paint is to _____.

   picture
   brush

6. Thermometer is to temperature
   as clock is to

   _____.

   time
   hour

7. Chick is to hen
   as kitten is to _____.

   cat
   cute

8. Toe is to foot as finger is to

   _____.

   nail
   hand

Name _____

Cross out the word that does not belong. Then write a word from the word box that does belong. Write a title above each list.

flute	Seattle	division	daffodil	motorcycle	noun

1. _____

sunflower	rose
daisy	tulip
lettuce	carnation

_____

2. _____

fraction	sentence
equals	addition
subtraction	multiplication

_____

3. _____

trombone	drums
cherry	piano
guitar	violin

_____

4. _____

comma	period
colon	pronoun
verb	seven

_____

5. _____

scooter	car
bike	toaster
skateboard	truck

_____

6. _____

New York	Dallas
Paris	London
marker	Chicago

_____

Name _____

Complete each analogy with a word from the word box.

footprint	run
condensation	light
darkness	bacteria
stomach	chameleon

A WORM IS TO A FISH AS A CHEESEBURGER IS TO A FIFTH GRADER!

HEY DUDE— WHERE'S THE FRIES?

1. Warm-blooded is to cold-blooded as a bear is to a _____.

2. Gravity is to weightlessness as light is to _____.

3. Ear is to sound as eye is to _____.

4. Bird is to fly as cheetah is to _____.

5. Dinosaur is to fossil as shoe is to _____.

6. Telescope is to planets as microscope is to _____.

7. Lifeless is to living as evaporation is to _____.

8. Blood vessel is to heart as intestine is to _____.

Name _____

Complete each analogy.

1. **Lead** is to **pencil** as **ink** is to _____.

2. **Foot** is to **sock** as **head** is to _____.

3. **Scoop** is to **ice cream** as **slice** is to _____.

4. **Hot** is to **summer** as **cold** is to _____.

5. **Rain** is to **wet** as **sunshine** is to _____.

6. **Smile** is to **happy** as **cry** is to _____.

7. **Dark** is to **black** as **light** is to _____.

8. **Earring** is to **ear** as **necklace** is to _____.

9. **Calf** is to **cow** as **kitten** is to _____.

10. **Airplane** is to **fly** as **car** is to _____.

11. **Snake** is to **slither** as **ant** is to _____.

12. **Cheetah** is to **fast** as **snail** is to _____.

Name _____

Synonyms are words that mean the **same** thing.
   Cute and **adorable** are **synonyms**.

Circle the synonyms for the first word in each row.

1. fast   quick   hard   swift   speedy   small

2. bright   dazzling   dull   glittering   sparkling

3. friend   stranger   companion   chum   pal   buddy

4. scary   scream   frightening   rough   terrifying

5. throw   fling   carry   hurl   toss   catch

Look at the picture below. Using the words you circled write a list of synonyms to describe each picture.

   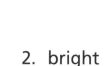

1. fast

_____

_____

_____

2. bright

_____

_____

_____

3. friend

_____

_____

_____

_____

4. scary

_____

_____

5.throw

_____

_____

_____

Name _____

Choose the word from the word box that could replace the **boldfaced** word in each sentence. Write the word on the line.

fortunate	discovered	grimy	ancient
sizzling	entire	select	chuckle

1. The dinosaur bones were **old**.

_____

2. We were **lucky** that it didn't rain.

_____

3. After playing football, my clothes were **dirty**.

_____

4. That joke made me **laugh**.

_____

5. I rode my bike the **whole** way home.

_____

6. I had to **choose** a book for my report

_____

7. It was a **hot** day in the desert.

_____

8. I **found** the missing puzzle piece on the floor.

_____

Name _____

Use the words from the word box to write a synonym for each underlined word.

| enjoyable |
| receive |
| also |
| scorching |
| most |
| friend |
| tease |
| like |
| happy |
| watching |

Dear Pen Pal,

I was glad _____

to get _____

your letter. Soccer is my

favorite sport too _____.

And I have three brothers who

always bother _____

me, too! Seattle sounds like a great _____ place to live, but I

wouldn't enjoy _____ all the rain. It's always sunny and hot

_____ in Houston. My friends and I like viewing

_____ movies and going out for ice cream afterwards. I like

chocolate best _____.

Your Pal _____ ,

_____

Name _____

Circle the two words in each row that are synonyms.

1. mistake   error   repair

2. rich   money   wealthy

3. frighten   startle   secret

4. song   noisy   loud

5. imitate   copy   return

6. hasty   funny   speedy

7. cheap   expensive   inexpensive

8. break   repair   fix

9. travel   vacation   work

10. gift   present   watch

11. friend   enemy   pal

12. watch   see   mean

Name _____

Answer the clues using words from the word box to complete the puzzle.

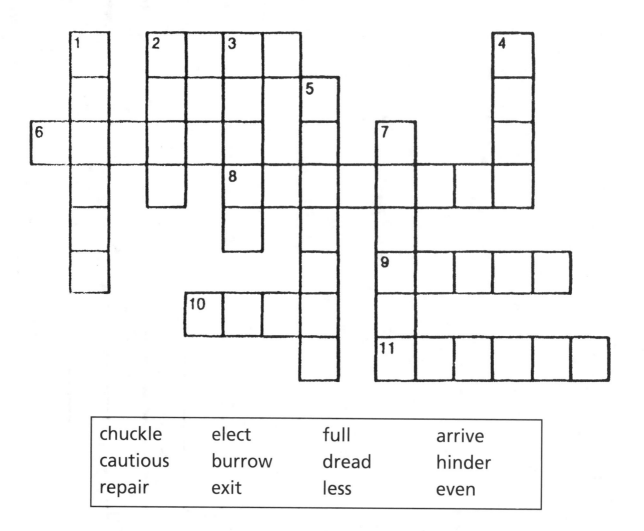

chuckle	elect	full	arrive
cautious	burrow	dread	hinder
repair	exit	less	even

Across

2. synonym for same
6. synonym for come
8. synonym for careful
9. synonym for fear
10. synonym for crowded
11. synonym for fix

Down

1. synonym for dig
2. synonym for leave
3. synonym for choose
4. synonym for fewer
5. synonym for laugh
7. synonym for obstruct

Name _____

An **antonym** is a word that means the **opposite**.

Answer the clues using words from the word box to complete the puzzle.

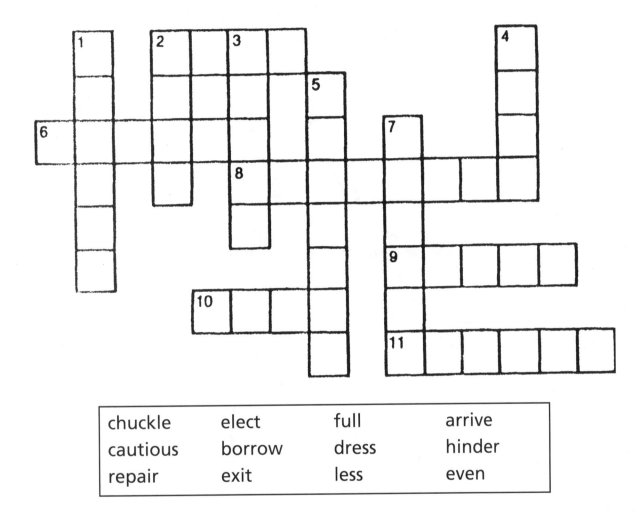

chuckle	elect	full	arrive
cautious	borrow	dress	hinder
repair	exit	less	even

Across
2. antonym for odd
6. antonym for depart
8. antonym for careless
9. antonym for undress
10. antonym for empty
11. antonym for break

Down
1. antonym for lend
2. antonym for enter
3. antonym for impeach
4. antonym for more
5. antonym for cry
7. antonym for help

Name _____

Write an antonym
on the line to
complete each sentence.

Dear Pen Pal,

I have something exciting

to _____ you!
      ask

Yesterday we went to

the animal shelter. I

_____
lost

old	select
big	cute
play	wild
female	hard
tell	loves
baby	friend
found	long

three kittens that were _____. It was _____ to
                ugly   easy

decide which one to _____. I chose a _____ kitten.
                      refuse   male

She is six weeks _____. She has _____ white fur
                young   short

with a _____ black spot on her face. She _____ to
        small   hates

_____ with a tissue on a string. She acts like a _____
work   tame

tiger. We made a cozy bed for her in a box. My _____ sister gave
                            adult

her a warm blanket for her box. I'll send you a picture of my cat soon. Do you

have any pets?

Your _____ ,
          enemy

_____

Circle the two words in each row that have opposite meanings.

1. return   break   fix

2. rich   poor   wealth

3. light   sun   dark

4. loud   nosy   quiet

5. borrow   lend   reduce

6. haste   slow   speedy

7. cheap   expensive   silly

8. watch   break   repair

9. travel   play   work

10. lost   found   cook

11. write   buy   sell

12. kind   friendly   mean

Name _____

Write an antonym for each word.

1. son   _____

2. lost   _____

3. chilly   _____

4. whole   _____

5. speak   _____

6. sent   _____

7. bare   _____

8. won   _____

9. male   _____

10. high   _____

11. sell   _____

12. girl   _____

13. dark   _____

14. empty   _____

15. inside   _____

Name _____

Each sentence below was meant to say the opposite. Circle the incorrect word in each sentence. Choose a word from the word box to replace it. Rewrite each sentence using the new word.

sad	after	hard	odd	apart	borrow

1. I chipped a tooth on the soft candy.

   _____

2. Three and five are even numbers.

   _____

3. My puzzle pieces fell together.

   _____

4. June comes before May.

   _____

5. I was happy when my friend moved.

   _____

6. May I lend your eraser?

   _____

Name _____

Homonyms are words that **sound similar** but **mean different things** and are sometimes **spelled differently**.

Write the missing word in each sentence.

| way |
| weigh |

1. How much does the puppy _____?
2. Which _____ do you walk home?

| not |
| knot |

3. I am _____ going to be late.
4. Can you untie the _____?

| our |
| hour |

5. That is _____ house.
6. We will be home in an _____.

| eight |
| ate |

7. He _____ two hot dogs.
8. There are _____ people here.

| here |
| hear |

9. Did you _____ the news?
10. Put the letter in _____.

| too |
| two |

11. Can you come _____?
12. She has _____ sisters.

| bee |
| be |

13. I was stung by a _____.
14. Will you _____ home at three?

| pair |
| pear |

15. Pick a _____ from the tree.
16. I need a new _____ of shoes.

Name _____

Choose the correct word to complete each sentence. Then write the meaning of the word you chose on the line below the sentence.

 **desert** — very dry land

dessert — after-meal treat

1. Dad made us pudding for a

    special _____.

2. We drove across miles of sandy

    _____.

 **lose** — misplace

loose — not tight

3. My brother's sweater was too

    _____.

4. The money is in my pocket so I

    won't _____ it.

single — only, one

signal — warning sign

5. The _____

    letter in the mailbox was for me.

6. The red light was a

    _____ to stop.

Read the list below. Two different meanings are given for each word.

iris	1) a type of flower	2) colored part of the eye
perch	1) a type of fish	2) a bird's resting place
bill	1) notice of money owed	2) a bird's beak
trunk	1) storage area of car	2) an elephant's nose
ruler	1) a person who governs	2) a tool for measuring
spring	1) to leap forward	2) a coil of wire
log	1) a daily record	2) section of a tree

Decide which meaning the **boldfaced** word has in each sentence below. Then write the meaning on the line.

1. I had enough money to pay the **bill**.

   _____

2. We put the suitcases in the **trunk**.

   _____

3. You'll need a **ruler** to check the length.

   _____

4. Keep a **log** of your progress.

   _____

5. A purple **iris** is growing in the garden.

   _____

6. The clock needs a new **spring**.

   _____

7. Put another **log** on the fire.

   _____

8. I think I caught a **perch**.

   _____

9. She was the nation's **ruler**.

   _____

10. A duck has an orange **bill**.

   _____

Spectrum Vocabulary Grade 5

Name _____

Read the pairs of homonyms in the word box. Read the story below and circle each incorrect word. Then rewrite the story using the correct words.

know	for	threw	sale	flour	rolls	isle	pairs
no	four	through	sail	flower	roles	aisle	pears
by	one	cereal	beats	weekly	steak	There	so
buy	won	serial	beets	weakly	stake	Their	sew

In the Bag

It was time four the weakly grocery shopping. Dad takes me because I no a good by when I see won. We walked threw every isle looking for what was on sail. Their were specials on stake, serial, pairs, flower, beats, and roles, sew we stocked up!

_____

_____

_____

_____

_____

_____

_____

Name _____

Rewrite each sentence using the correct homonym.

1. My Ant Betty always bakes the Thanksgiving turkey.

   _____

2. Tim caught the fowl ball and threw it back to the pitcher.

   _____

3. Mom used the smelly chemical when ceiling the basement walls.

   _____

4. That banned played at the school picnic.

   _____

5. You are such a deer to help me carry in the groceries.

   _____

6. The weatherman says this reign will last a few more days.

   _____

Name _____

Read the pairs of words in the word box. Then read the story below. Circle the incorrect words. Then rewrite the story using the right words.

road	waist	lone	weight	by
rode	waste	loan	wait	buy

Land of His Own

The cowboy road his horse into town. He didn't waist any time getting there. He went to the bank to get a lone. He had to weight awhile. But soon he had money to by land of his own!

_____

_____

_____

_____

_____

_____

Name _____

Context clues are clues you can find in a sentence to help you figure out **what a word means**.

Write the letter of the best meaning of the <u>underlined</u> word on the line before each sentence.

1. _____ The gardener planted the flowers in a <u>bed</u> that would get lots of sunshine.

2. _____ The <u>bed</u> of coals glowed orange and yellow in the darkness. It was perfect for roasting marshmallows.

3. _____ Terri jumped into <u>bed</u> and pulled the covers up to her chin. She curled up and began reading her book.

    A. a piece of furniture used for sleeping   B. a plot of ground prepared for plants   C. a flat layer

4. _____ Nancy rounded third base and ran for home <u>plate</u>.

5. _____ Maclin took the photographic <u>plate</u> to the printer so the newspaper could be published.

6. _____ George put salad and a burger on his <u>plate</u>.

    A. a smooth, flat, thin piece of material   B. a dish to eat from   C. a square bag to mark a place

7. _____ Please <u>match</u> the sentence with the best answer.

8. _____ The class was watching the tennis <u>match</u>.

9. _____ Gail lit the <u>match</u>. She used it to light the birthday candles.

    A. a contest   B. a small stick with a flammable material on the end used to start a fire   C. put together into a pair

Name _____

Choose the best meaning for the underlined word as used in the sentence. Write a checkmark on the line next to your choice.

1. As Meg walked out of the room, she turned the <u>switch</u> to off and the light went out.
   _____ A. to change from one thing to another
   _____ B. something used to turn off and on lights
   _____ C. a slender, flexible rod or twig

2. Dad told the children that they should have <u>minded</u> him. If they had, the bikes would not have been stolen.
   _____ A. something you think with
   _____ B. to dig minerals out of the earth
   _____ C. to follow someone's directions

3. Jean carefully removed the wax from the <u>mold</u>. Each candle was shaped like a star.
   _____ A. a form for making something into a certain shape
   _____ B. a fuzzy growth
   _____ C. the surface of the earth

4. Alex moved the <u>dash</u> up and down. It became harder to move as the cream turned into butter.
   _____ A. a short line
   _____ B. to run very quickly
   _____ C. the handle of the butter churn

5. Mom put a little <u>pat</u> of butter on the side of the plate.
   _____ A. to gently pet or tap
   _____ B. someone's name
   _____ C. a small individual portion

6. Choose two underlined words and write them on the lines below. Then use them in sentences. Use different definitions than the ones used in the sentences above.

   _____   _____

   _____

   _____

Name _____

Circle the word(s) that is closest in meaning to the <u>underlined</u> word.

1. Cheryl's umbrella hat was so <u>peculiar</u> looking that everyone in the entire park stared over at it!

       bright   large   unusual

2. Sandra insisted on being <u>prompt</u> for the concert because she didn't want to miss a single minute of the performance.

       on time   late   ready to laugh

3. David's pet rabbit is so <u>brilliant</u> that it even asks to help make the dinner salad!

       available   rich   incredibly smart

4. The kids on Amanda's new street were so <u>considerate</u> that they introduced themselves on the day she moved in.

       rude   fortunate   polite

5. Mark wanted to catch the same kind of butterfly that Jeff did so badly that he asked everyone if there were any more in the <u>vicinity</u>.

       house   area   shopping mall

6. The watermelon from Curt's garden was so <u>enormous</u> that he had to use a wheelbarrow to carry it into the house!

       gigantic   colorful   funny-shaped

7. Michele caught a <u>glimpse</u> of the new swimming pool as she rode her bike past the gate.

       taste   understanding   quick look

8. Eva's poodle <u>clenched</u> the stick in its teeth.

       grabbed tightly   chewed   scratched

9. Because there was such a <u>variety</u> of kites to choose from, Jolie had no idea what to buy!

       large selection   mess   small amount

10. Cyndi was very <u>apprehensive</u> about buying the iguana until she found out that iguanas are herbivorous!

        happy   excited   unsure

11. After Peter finished making the bread, he realized he had left out one of the most important <u>ingredients</u> — the yeast!

        cooking utensil   color   part of the mixture

12. Monica was amazed at the perfectly shaped <u>hexagons</u> that the bees had made in their hive.

        flower bouquets   6-sided polygons   honey treats

Name _____

Read each sentence carefully. Write a short definition for each <u>underlined</u> word.

1. A child <u>fidgeted</u> uncomfortably on the bench.

   _____

2. After losing her wallet, Mattie was on the <u>brink</u> of tears.

   _____

3. In the smoky, smog-filled neighborhood, the jogger <u>yearned</u> for clean air.

   _____

4. Mike became more <u>upbeat</u> after finishing his homework and started working on his model airplane.

   _____

5. The friends became <u>somber</u> when Renee announced that her family was moving to Wisconsin.

   _____

6. Penny felt <u>sluggish</u> after helping her mom in the garden all day.

   _____

Circle the word which best completes each sentence.

1. Kevin slowly picked up his _____ to play the Chopin nocturne.

   toothpick   clarinet
   piano

2. With fearful trepidation, he lifted the mouthpiece to his _____.

   ears   chest   lips

3. Out of the bell of his reed instrument came a _____ squawk.

   horrendous   peaceful   loving

4. Mrs. Dee Canon abruptly lowered her _____.

   button   shoe   baton

5. "Who so shockingly _____ in a goose from his or her barnyard?" she asked.

   brought   danced   cooked

6. Feeling so _____ he could have hidden under his chair, Kevin raised his hand.

   daring   awful   sleepy

7. Forty-two pairs of eyes turned to stare at the _____-red face of this would-be Benny Goodman.

   potato   beet   celery

8. Mrs. Canon, noting Kevin's chagrin, calmly regained the attention of her _____.

   ears   clarinet   class

9. "Who can tell me the last time they didn't make a rude sound with a _____ instrument?" she began.

   scientific   musical   electronic

10. "Oh," entered Sean _____, "I remember that four months ago Sunday I didn't make a mistake."

    understandingly   madly   cryptically

11. "And _____ was that?" asked Mrs. Canon, amused by Sean's wisdom.

    who   what   why

12. "Well, you know, we didn't get our instruments until the next _____," replied Sean.

    Christmas   pizza   Monday

13. Mrs. Canon looked at every band member who _____ and nodded their heads.

    hollered   smiled   marched

14. "Kevin," she said softly, "you're doing fine. My goodness! I _____ on my trumpet for two years solid. Just ask my mother."

    squealed   stepped   played

15. Kevin almost smiled, though he kept his head _____.

    nodding   askew   lowered

16. Raising her baton once more, Mrs. Canon returned to the nocturne, and the _____ played on.

    game   band   toys

Read the passage carefully. Find and write a **boldfaced** word from the passage for each description below.

Computer Data

Computers may seem "smart" but they cannot think. The only thing they can do is follow a set of instructions called a **program** which must be written by a person. The computer **hardware** (machinery) and **software** (programs) work together.

For the computer to work, a person must enter **data**, or information, into the computer. This is called **input**. New data is entered by typing on a **keyboard** that has letters and symbols like a typewriter. Data may be stored on a **disk** which is used to record and save information.

Next, the computer "reads" the data and follows the instructions of the program. The program may tell it to organize the data, compare it to other data, or store it for later use. This is called data **processing**.

When the processing is complete, the computer can display the results either on the screen or printed on paper as a **printout**.

1. _____ used to save and record information

2. _____ organizing, comparing, or storing data

3. _____ results printed on paper

4. _____ set of instructions for a computer

5. _____ computer machinery

6. _____ entering data

7. _____ computer programs

8. _____ where data is entered

Name _____

Concept words are words that have to do with a
certain **topic** or **idea**. Complete the puzzle on page 33
using the clues and the word box below.

Across

3. An _____ is the darkening of one heavenly body by another.

5. The gas that we need in order to live is called _____.

6. An _____ eats both plants and animals.

10. A _____ eats only plants.

11. The _____ contains all the colors of the rainbow and white light.

Down

1. _____ is the process by which plants use carbon dioxide and sunlight to make food.

2. An _____ studies the different celestial bodies.

4. A frozen mass of dust and ice with a long tail that travels around the sun is called a _____.

7. The air that surrounds the earth is called our _____.

8. A _____ is two or more atoms joined together.

9. A _____ eats only meat.

photosynthesis	carnivore	eclipse
spectrum	herbivore	oxygen
atmosphere	omnivore	comet
astronomer	molecule	

Name _____

Name _____

Many interesting words are based on Greek and Roman mythology.

Read the names and descriptions of the gods and goddesses below. Then use this information to help you match the letter beside the English word to the correct definition. Write the letters in the blanks.

Sol—Roman sun god
Luna—Roman goddess of the moon
Mars—Roman god of war

Faunus—Roman god of animals
Ceres—Roman goddess of agriculture, especially grains
Hygeia—Greek goddess of health

Definition	*English word*
1. _____ animals of a particular region	**a. martial**
2. _____ relating to military or war	**b. hygiene**
3. _____ any food made from grain, such as wheat, oats, or rice	**c. solar**
4. _____ practice of good health habits	**d. lunar**
5. _____ having to do with the sun	**e. fauna**
6. _____ relating to the moon	**f. cereal**

Write one of the six English words above to complete each sentence below.

7. The nurses went to the villages to teach better _____.

8. The _____ panels collect energy from the sun.

9. Many young people learn karate, one of the _____ arts.

10. The wildlife expert was making a study of the park's _____.

11. The student ate a breakfast of milk and _____.

12. Tonight, there will be a _____ eclipse.

Name _____

Write the state for each capital. Use a map to help you.

Montpelier
_____

Cheyenne
_____

Tallahassee
_____

Madison
_____

Springfield
_____

Denver
_____

Jefferson City
_____

Albany
_____

Salem
_____

Sacramento
_____

Atlanta
_____

Baton Rouge
_____

Pierre
_____

Austin
_____

Lansing
_____

Name _____

Complete each sentence with a word from the word box. Then complete the puzzle.

1.
2.
3.
4.
5.
6.
7.
8.

| count |
| add |
| numbers |
| plus |
| minus |
| equals |
| even |
| odd |

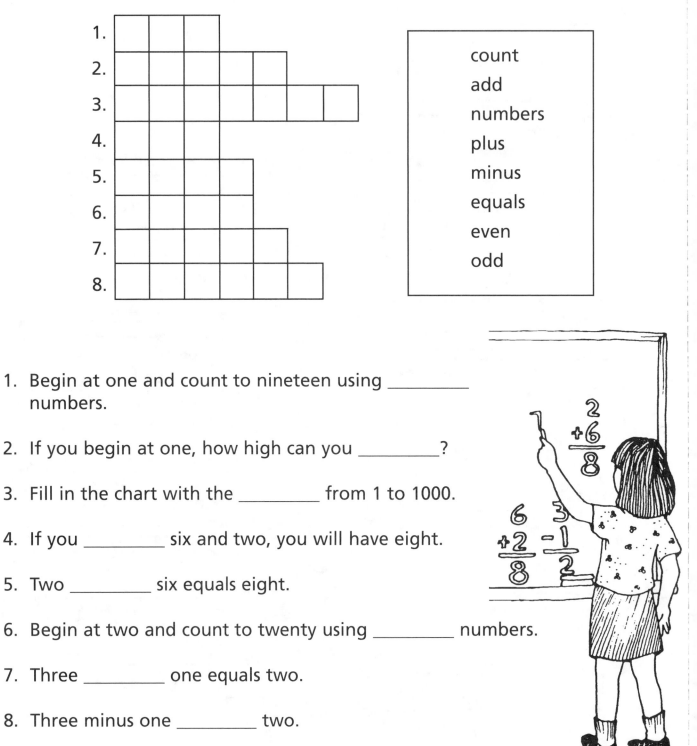

1. Begin at one and count to nineteen using _____ numbers.

2. If you begin at one, how high can you _____?

3. Fill in the chart with the _____ from 1 to 1000.

4. If you _____ six and two, you will have eight.

5. Two _____ six equals eight.

6. Begin at two and count to twenty using _____ numbers.

7. Three _____ one equals two.

8. Three minus one _____ two.

Name _____

Read the passage carefully.

Many children like to take part in games because they enjoy the **action** of a sport.

In tennis class, they learn to **volley** the ball, hitting it back quickly before it touches the ground. They **warm up** before the games to get ready for a **match**. Their teachers, or **coaches**, encourage them to do their best. In tennis, **deuce** means the score is tied at 40, so the players have to work hard to score the next two points to get ahead. When they become good players, people may come to watch them play.

Write the **boldfaced** words next to their meanings in the tennis balls below.

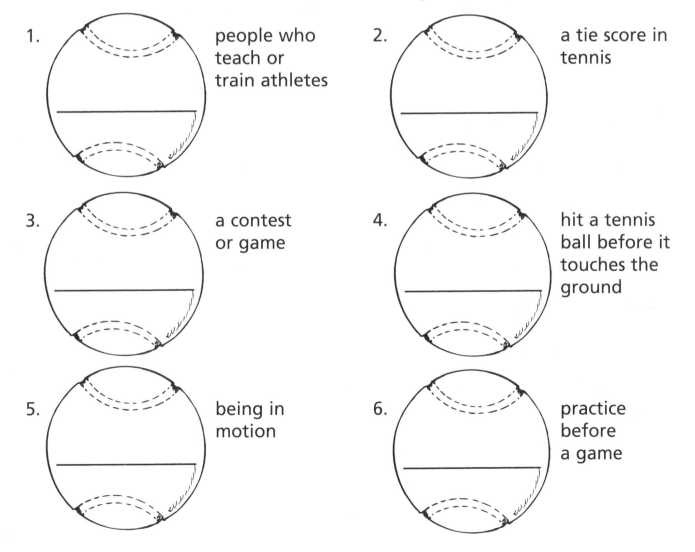

1. people who teach or train athletes

2. a tie score in tennis

3. a contest or game

4. hit a tennis ball before it touches the ground

5. being in motion

6. practice before a game

Name _____

A **sensory word** describes something you **smell, touch, taste, see,** or **hear**. Write a word from the word box that describes the phrase.

```
pop
growl
buzz
bang
splash
squeak
clop
cock-a-doodle-doo
```

1. a horse's hooves on the pavement _____

2. popcorn in the microwave _____

3. a mouse behind the stove _____

4. a kid in a puddle of water _____

5. a rooster at dawn _____

6. a bee around a flower _____

7. a door slamming _____

8. a dog showing its teeth _____

Name _____

Match the sense with the sensory word.

see	salty
touch	quiet
hear	sticky
smell	dark
taste	sour

Write a sentence using each of the sensory words above.

1. _____

2. _____

3. _____

4. _____

5. _____

Name _____

Rewrite each sentence using at least two sensory words.

1. Can you hear that?

   _____

2. Look at that!

   _____

3. This is my project.

   _____

4. This book is good.

   _____

5. My friend is nice.

   _____

Name _____

Read the cues in the word box. Write a paragraph answering each cue. Use sensory words to develop your ideas.

My favorite . . .	I am . . .	I ate . . .	I play . . .
My friend . . .	I feel . . .	I study . . .	I like . . .

_____

_____

_____

_____

_____

_____

_____

_____

_____

_____

Name _____

Onomatopoeia is a word that **sounds like** the sound it describes. Read each onomatopoeia word. Write a sentence describing the cause of the noise.

1. slop

    _____

    _____

2. murmur

    _____

    _____

3. fizz

    _____

    _____

4. knock

    _____

    _____

5. whine

    _____

    _____

6. thunk

    _____

    _____

Name _____

A **plural** is **more than one** of a person, place, or thing. Remember
        Change **y** to **i** and add **es**
        Words that end in **sh, ch, x,** or **z** add **es**
        Change **f** to **v** and add **es**

Change each word to the plural form. Write the word on the line.

1. The _____ are pretty colors.
               leaf

2. We picked _____ in the woods.
               berry

3. We saw a movie about _____.
               wolf

4. The _____ are in the barn.
               calf

5. There are two _____ in the city.
               library

6. Dad built _____ in the garage.
               shelf

7. It costs a dollar to ride the _____.
               pony

8. The story is about seven tiny _____.
               elf

9. _____ are fun to watch at night.
               Firefly

10. Mother planted _____ in the yard.
               lily

11. The mother lion has three _____.
               baby

12. The police caught the _____.
               thief

Name _____

Make the following words plural.

1. cranberry _____

2. bunny _____

3. calf _____

4. church _____

5. rainbow _____

6. watch _____

7. life _____

8. hobby _____

9. notch _____

10. vicinity _____

11. psalm _____

12. index _____

13. half _____

14. suffix _____

15. symphony _____

Name _____

Make the following words plural by adding **s** or **es**.

1. ostrich _____
2. buffalo _____
3. camper _____
4. balloon _____
5. toothbrush _____
6. birch _____
7. caterpillar _____
8. lunch _____
9. tomato _____
10. paragraph _____
11. skateboard _____
12. volcano _____
13. potato _____
14. class _____
15. sandbox _____
16. notebook _____
17. fossil _____

BUFFALO?
AIN'T THAT NEAR
ROCHESTER?

Name _____

Write the plural of each word on the line. Then write the plural in the correct box puzzle.

1. match _____

2. city _____

3. school _____

4. foot _____

5. body _____

6. church _____

7. man _____

8. radio _____

9. calf _____

10. penny _____

11. child _____

12. piano _____

13. woman _____

14. story _____

15. sandwich _____

16. mouse _____

Name _____

A **suffix** is a word part added to the **end of a word** to change its meaning.

-ist A noun-forming suffix, -ist means a person who makes, does, or practices.	**-ly** An adverb- or adjective-forming suffix, -ly means when, how, like, or in the manner of.
-less An adjective-forming suffix, -less means without or lacking.	**-fy** A verb-forming suffix, -fy means to make or cause to be or become.
-ness A noun-forming suffix, -ness means state or quality of being.	**-ize** A verb-forming suffix, -ize means to cause to be or to become.

From the following list, select the correct word to complete each sentence. Write the word on the line.

vaporize   naturalist   harshly   purify   pitiless   correctness

1. Before drinking river water you should _____ it because it may be polluted.

2. A person who practices the study of nature is a _____.

3. The _____ football coach made the team run an extra mile.

4. Check your spelling for _____ when using new words.

5. The angry man spoke _____ to the telephone operator.

6. High temperatures will make water _____.

Use the suffixes in the word box to make new words that answer each phrase. Write the word on the line.

7. An adjective meaning without power. _____

8. An adverb that tells how a brave person acts. _____

9. A verb meaning to make simple. _____

10. A noun meaning a person who makes works of art. _____

11. A verb meaning to form crystals. _____

12. A noun meaning the state of being dark. _____

Name _____

Use the word box to fill in the blanks with words containing suffixes. Put each boxed letter in the matching numbered blank below to find out the state you might visit to get something necessary for school.

invitation	penniless	wonderful	hopeless
careful	noisy	collection	peaceful
addition	followed	winning	

1. h __ ☐ __ __ __ __ s

2. ☐ __ d __ t __ __ __

3. __ __ ☐ __ __ w __ d

4. w __ __ ☐ __ __

5. w __ ☐ d __ __ __ __ __ __

6. __ ☐ r __ f __ __

7. i __ ☐ __ t __ __ __ __

8. c __ __ __ __ e ☐ __ __

9. ☐ __ i __ y

10. __ __ a __ ☐ __ __ l

11. __ __ n n ☐ __ __ __ __

$\overline{}$ $\overline{}$ $\overline{}$ $\overline{}$ $\overline{}$ $\overline{}$ — $\overline{}$ $\overline{}$ $\overline{}$ $\overline{}$ $\overline{}$
1 10 5 8 11 3   7 2 9 4 6

Name _____

The suffix **able** means *capable of*. For example, a wire that is **bendable** can bend.

Add **able** to the words below. (If a word ends in a silent e, you may need to drop the e before adding a suffix beginning with a vowel.)

break_____   notice_____   reason_____

The suffixes **en** and **ize** mean *to make* or *cause to be*. Add **en** to the words below.

bright_____   hard_____   sharp_____

Add **ize** to the words below.

modern_____   tender_____   sterile_____

The suffix **ist** means *one who does something*. Add **ist** to the words below.

type_____   violin_____   perfection_____

The suffix **ous** means *having the quality of*. Add **ous** to the words below.

marvel_____   nerve_____   courage_____

Use the words you wrote above to complete the sentences below.

1. Pat's answer was so _____, everyone agreed she must be right.

2. The soldier received a medal for his _____ act in battle.

3. We went to the concert to listen to my favorite _____.

4. In a hospital, someone must _____ instruments that are used in operations.

5. My friends who read that novel said that it was _____!

6. Mrs. Grant wants to _____ her kitchen by replacing the old cupboard doors.

7. Painting this room white will help to _____ its appearance.

8. Mr. Burns is such a _____ that he will redo his work many times over.

9. Before a test, try to stay calm and not get _____.

10. If you display the bulletin on this wall, it will be more _____.

11. Clay will _____ and be difficult to mold if you leave it out.

12. Try not to drop the vase because it is _____.

Name _____

Read the passage carefully.

"The treasure must be in here!" yelled Brad. He and his sister Lauren stood outside the **entrance** of a cave. As Brad took a step towards the **darkness**, Lauren touched his arm.

"Let's rest a bit," said Lauren, still **breathless** from running. "Besides, it might be **dangerous** in there."

Brad held up a tattered notebook that had *Abigail* etched faintly on its cover. "This diary we found says Abigail hid a treasure in here," he said. "I want to find it before anyone else does." Brad turned and stepped inside the cave with **determination**. Lauren sighed and **reluctantly** followed her brother.

Brad waved his flashlight impatiently around the cave. Moments later he cried, "I see something!" Brad stooped down and started digging in the earth with a rock. Lauren came to help. Soon the two uncovered a small **wooden** box. Brad's hands shook with **excitement**. He took the box outside and opened it. Brad and Lauren gasped and looked at the contents in **astonishment**. Inside were letters addressed to Abigail.

"Nothing but letters!" moaned Brad with **disappointment**. "There's no treasure here at all." He sank to the ground feeling tired and a bit **foolish**.

Lauren stood with a **thoughtful** look on her face. "If it's any **consolation**," she said slowly, "we did find Abigail's treasure." Lauren fingered the letters **gently** and continued, "These letters were written by someone whose **friendship** Abigail felt very strongly about. She probably put the letters in the cave for safekeeping."

Write the **boldfaced** words beside their meanings below. Circle the suffix in each word.

1. place of entry_____

2. out of breath _____

3. state of being excited _____

4. having little or no light_____

5. great surprise_____

6. unwise _____

7. deep in thought _____

8. state of being friends_____

9. with unwillingness _____

10. act of being comforted _____

11. feeling let down _____

12. quality of being firm _____

13. in a gentle manner_____

14. made of wood_____

15. involving something that can

    cause harm _____

Name _____

Read the passage carefully.

Alina and Melissa arrived home after playing at their friend's house. It was only seven o'clock, but **darkness** had already fallen. The porch lights were on, offering a **cheery** welcome to the two sisters.

"It was fun playing Megan's new video game," said Alina as she and Melissa walked up the driveway.

"It sure was," agreed Melissa. Suddenly she stopped and touched her sister's arm. "What's that?" she whispered in a **fearful** voice.

Alina followed her sister's gaze. There by the steps leading to their front door was a plump, furry creature with a **bushy** tail and **beady** eyes. At first the girls thought it was a large cat, but they realized they were wrong when they noticed the animal's thin snout.

"It's an opossum!" gasped Alina in **amazement**. "Don't move. It might be **dangerous**."

The girls stared at the animal, making no noise or **movement**. How they wished they could be inside their safe, **comfortable** home! Alina and Melissa yearned to take the few quick steps needed to reach the front door and **freedom**, but they knew a move like that could **frighten** the opossum. So the girls waited, each hopeful that their unexpected **visitor** would get tired and leave. If they were not so worried, their situation might have appeared **comical** to them.

After what seemed hours, the opossum turned and scurried into the blackness. "I'm glad he's gone," said Alina with a sigh of relief. "For awhile, I was **doubtful** he would ever leave!"

"Me, too," said Melissa. "Come on, let's go inside before he decides to visit us again!"

Write the **boldfaced** words beside their meanings below. Circle the suffix in each word.

1. able to cause harm_____

2. showing fear _____

3. bright and pleasant _____

4. thick and spreading _____

5. act of moving_____

6. a guest _____

7. state of comfort _____

8. small, round, and shiny _____

9. without light _____

10. cause to be afraid_____

11. great surprise_____

12. funny _____

13. not sure _____

14. state of being free _____

Name _____

The suffixes **ion** and **ity** mean the **state or quality of**. Add the suffix **ion** or **ity** to each word below.

1. the state of being protected   _____

2. the quality of being scarce   _____

3. the quality of being necessary   _____

4. the state of combining   _____

5. the state of colliding   _____

6. the state of being divided   _____

7. the state of being permitted   _____

8. the quality of being active   _____

9. the state of being received   _____

10. the state of being directed   _____

Name _____

A **prefix** is a part **added to the beginning** of a word to change its meaning. The prefix **un** means **not** and the prefix **re** means **again**. Add the correct prefix to each word in the word box. Write the new words in the correct column.

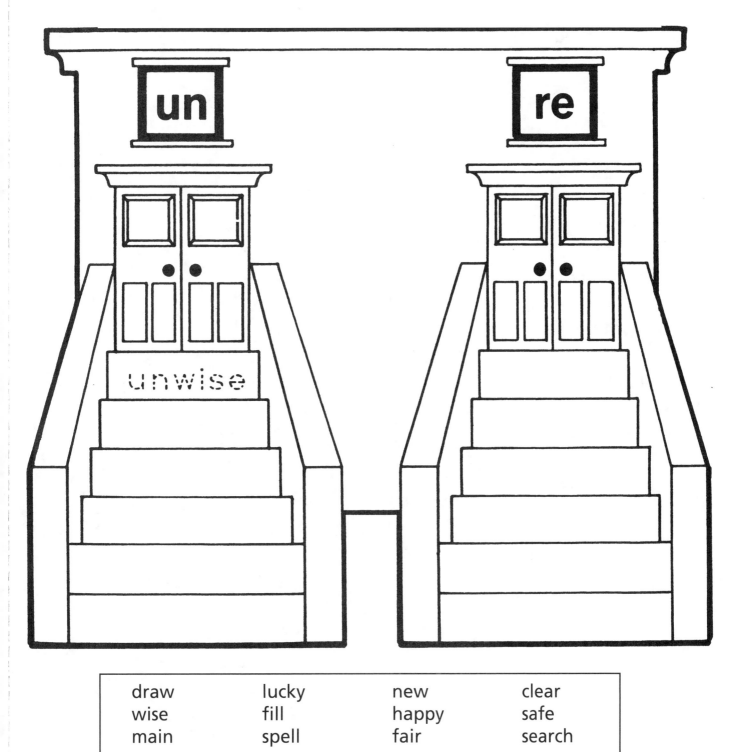

un — unwise

re

draw	lucky	new	clear
wise	fill	happy	safe
main	spell	fair	search

Name _____

Read each definition. Complete each sentence using a word with the prefix **un** or **re**.

1. I _____ my sled.
          painted again

2. Did you _____ your answer?
          consider again

3. Mei-Ling will _____ her poster.
          draw again

4. The treasure chest was _____.
          not locked

5. David's skates are _____.
          not laced

6. Grandfather likes to _____ that story.
          tell again

7. The writing was _____ and hard to read.
          not clear

8. Watch the _____ to see the touchdown.
          play again

9. How did she _____ the book report?
          do again

10. It is best to avoid _____ words.
           not kind

11. Jan will _____ the bookcase.
           finish again

12. The _____ stairway was marked with a sign.
           not safe

Name _____

The prefix **mis** means **wrongly** and the prefix **non** means **not**. Add the correct prefix to each word in the word box. Write the new words in the correct column.

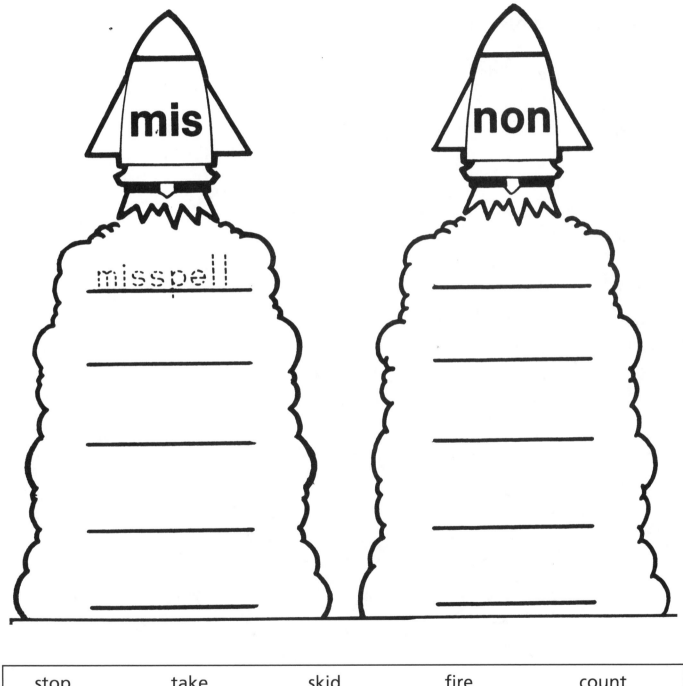

misspell

stop	take	skid	fire	count
spell	fat	place	sense	human

Name _____

The prefix **mis** means **wrongly** and the prefix **pre** means **before**.
Add the prefix to each word. Write the new word and then write its meaning.

Base Word	Prefix	New Word	Meaning
1. cook	pre	_____	_____
2. spell	mis	_____	_____
3. view	pre	_____	_____
4. school	pre	_____	_____
5. pay	pre	_____	_____
6. place	mis	_____	_____
7. use	mis	_____	_____
8. treat	mis	_____	_____

Name _____

The prefixes **im** and **dis** mean **not**. Add the correct prefix to each word in the word box. Write the new words in the correct column.

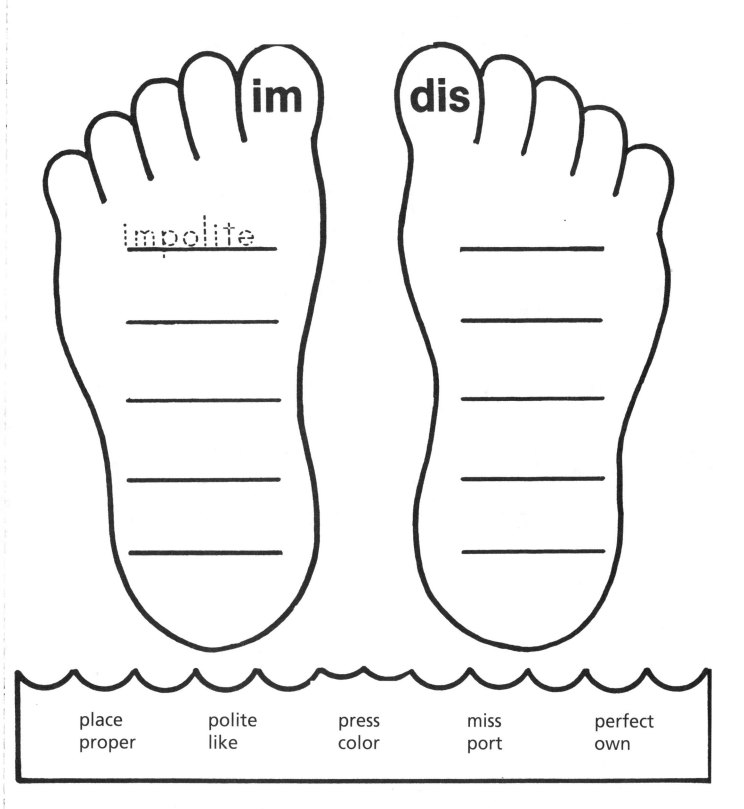

im

dis

impolite

| place | polite | press | miss | perfect |
| proper | like | color | port | own |

Name _____

Circle each word in the puzzle with a prefix. Write the words below. Circle the prefix.

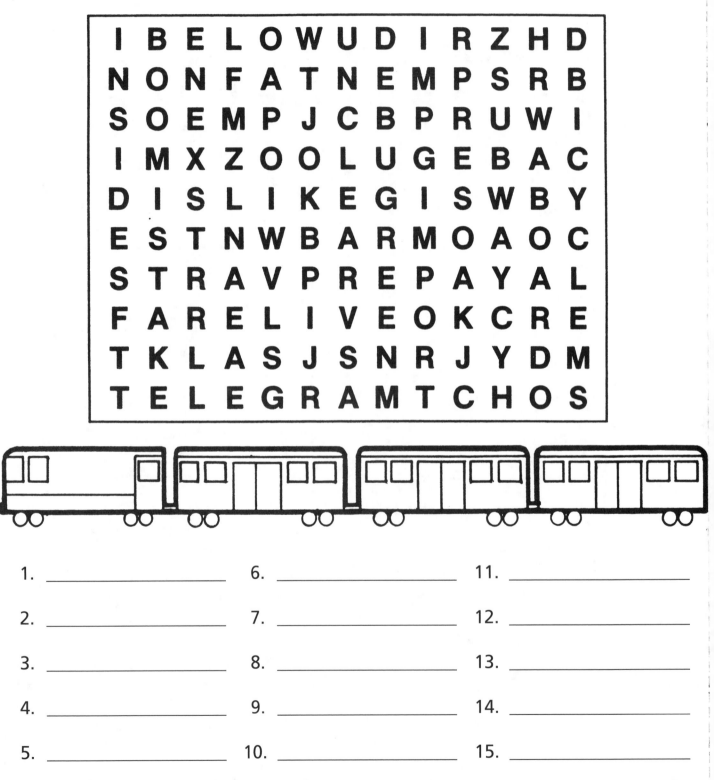

```
I B E L O W U D I R Z H D
N O N F A T N E M P S R B
S O E M P J C B P R U W I
I M X Z O O L U G E B A C
D I S L I K E G I S W B Y
E S T N W B A R M O A O C
S T R A V P R E P A Y A L
F A R E L I V E O K C R E
T K L A S J S N R J Y D M
T E L E G R A M T C H O S
```

1. _____   6. _____   11. _____

2. _____   7. _____   12. _____

3. _____   8. _____   13. _____

4. _____   9. _____   14. _____

5. _____   10. _____   15. _____

Name _____

Some words have Latin prefixes. Use the meanings of the Latin prefixes in the word box to help you write the English word for each definition below.

com	= together	**semi**	= half; partly	**dis**	= opposite
pre	= before	**re**	= back; again	**sub**	= below

1. a half circle _____

2. below zero _____

3. heat again _____

4. view before _____

5. opposite of agree _____

6. write again _____

7. gain back _____

8. partial darkness _____

9. press together _____

10. opposite of honest _____

11. appear again _____

12. opposite of respect _____

Name _____

A **root** or **base word** is the word that is left after you **take off a prefix or suffix**. Divide the following words into parts so the root is separate.

	auto	self
autobiography	the story of a person's life written by that person	
autograph	a person's signature or handwriting	
automatic	having a self-acting or self-regulating mechanism; done without thought or conscious effort	
automobile	a passenger vehicle with its own engine	
autonomous	self-governing	

1. automobile

   _____ _____

2. autobiography

   _____ _____

3. automatic

   _____ _____

4. autograph

   _____ _____

5. autonomous

   _____ _____

Complete each sentence using a word from the word box.

1. The writer finished the _____ about her life.

2. Sally got an _____ camera for her birthday.

3. Jose was excited when he got the celebrity's _____.

4. The people who lived on the island did not wish to be governed by a mother country any longer. They wanted to be _____.

Name _____

multi	many
multicolored	having many colors
multimedia	combining more than two artistic techniques or means of communication or expression, such as acting, lighting effects, and music
multimillionaire	a person who has at least two million dollars
multiple	having many parts or elements
multitude	a large number of persons or things

Unscramble the word and write the definition.

Example: limptule   multiple   having many parts or elements

1. rollutimedoc   _____   _____

2. lemonlimitailiur   _____   _____

3. demiltutu   _____   _____

4. immediatul   _____   _____

Complete each sentence using a word from the word box.

1. The unhappy result of John's skiing accident was a _____ fracture of the arm.

2. A kaleidoscope is constructed with _____ glass.

3. The rock concert with television screens and a light show was a _____ event.

4. A _____ donated money for the starving children.

5. The _____ of people followed the celebrity into the theater.

Name _____

pre	before
preamble	a statement that introduces a formal document, explaining its purpose
precede	to come or go before in rank, time, or order
prehistoric	of the period before written history
preoccupied	wholly occupied or absorbed in one's thoughts; absentminded
preschool	school before kindergarten; nursery school
prevent	to take action before an event to stop the event from happening

Write a short definition for each word.

Example: prehistoric   of the period before written history.

1. precede   _____

2. precedent   _____

3. preoccupation _____

4. prevention   _____

5. preventable   _____

Complete each sentence using a word from the word box.

1. The four-year-old child will attend a _____ class.

2. The dinosaurs lived during _____ times.

3. The teacher said we had to memorize the _____ to the United States Constitution.

4. Roger couldn't enjoy the movie because he was _____ about the test the next day.

5. Seventh grade _____(s) eighth grade.

Name _____

bi, di	two
biceps	any muscle having two points of origin
bilingual	able to use two languages equally well
biped	a two-footed animal
bisect	divide into two (usually equal) parts
dichromatic	having two colors
dilemma	a situation requiring a choice between two equal alternatives
diploma	a certificate awarded when a student has successfully completed a particular course of study
dipterous	having two wings

Complete each sentence using a word from the word box.

1. A fly is a _____ insect.
2. Lorenzo was taking a course in weight training, and would proudly flex his _____ when anyone asked how he was progressing.
3. Charlotte faced the _____ of whether to go to the movie with her friends or take the baby-sitting job.
4. Silvia is _____ because she speaks Spanish at home and English at school.
5. The geometry teacher told the students to _____ the circle.

Write a word with the prefix **bi** to complete each phrase.

1. *Annual* means once a year. _____ means twice a year.

2. A *biennium* is a two-year period. _____ means once every two years.

3. *Centum* is the Latin word for one hundred. _____ means once every two hundred years.

4. A _____ event happens twice a month.

5. A _____ event happens twice a week.

Name _____

ben, bene	good, well

benediction	a blessing
benefactor	a person who gives help or support, especially financial aid
beneficial	having a good or helpful effect
beneficiary	a person who receives a benefit or advantage, such as an inheritance
benevolent	doing good things; being good-hearted, kind
benign	gentle and kind; not threatening life

Fill in each blank with a word from the word box.

1. The musician needed a _____ to support him financially.

2. The priest said the _____ after the mass.

3. It is _____ to study vocabulary before taking a standardized test.

4. The _____ of his life insurance policy would receive $25,000.

5. My grandmother was very relieved when the tests showed that the tumor was _____.

Circle each word below in which **ben** or **bene** is used as a prefix meaning good, well.

beneath	Benelux
Benedict	benighted
benefactor	benignant
benefit	benumb

List five things that are beneficial to your health.

1. _____   2. _____

3. _____   4. _____

5. _____

Name _____

cred	to believe
accredit	to give credit for; to authorize or recognize officially
credence	acceptance or belief
credential	letter or document that proves or affirms a person's identity or right to hold a certain position
credo	a set of beliefs or opinions
credulous	inclined to believe anything, often without sufficient proof
discredit	to reject as untrue; to cast doubt on; to disgrace
incredible	unbelievable

Fill in each blank with a word from the word box.

1. His explanation for not having his homework was truly _____.

2. The golden rule is an important part of my _____.

3. Five years of college study are usually required to obtain a teaching _____.

4. Because they knew that enrollment had been dropping, they gave _____ to the rumor that the school would soon close.

5. Little Mikey was still _____; he would believe anything his big brothers told him.

6. The candidate's staff was trying hard to find ways to _____ the opponent.

Look up the following words and phrases in a dictionary and write a brief definition for each.

1. on credit_____

2. to one's credit_____

3. creditor_____

4. incredulous _____

5. credibility_____

hydr, hydro	water

dehydrate	to lose or remove water
hydrant	a large, upright pipe connected to a water main
hydraulics	being operated by or using a liquid
hydrocarbon	any of a large class of organic compounds that contain only carbon and hydrogen
hydroelectric	of or relating to electricity produced by the energy of flowing water, such as that from a dam
hydrophobia	an abnormal fear of water; rabies
hydroplane	a light, fast boat designed to skim along the surface of water; a seaplane

Fill in each blank with a word from the word box.

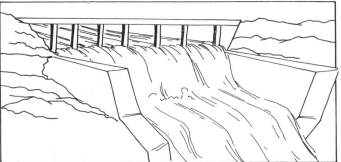

1. We crossed the English Channel in a _____.

2. To make raisins, you _____ grapes.

3. Hoover Dam is an important source of _____ power.

4. On extremely hot days, the mayor orders all _____(s) to be opened so that people can cool off in the water.

5. Because it causes an inability to swallow liquids, rabies is also known as _____.

Look up these hydro words in the dictionary. Write their meanings.

1. hydra _____

2. hydrogen _____

3. hydrolysis _____

4. hydroponics _____

5. hydrothermal _____

Name _____

Imported words are English words that **come from other languages,** such as German, French, or Latin.

Look up the following words in a dictionary. Write the definition in the blank beside each word.

1. **chef** (from French) _____

2. **chauffeur** (from French) _____

3. **petite** (from French) _____

4. **brocade** (from Spanish) _____

5. **pagoda** (from Portuguese) _____

6. **elite** (from French) _____

7. **menagerie** (from French) _____

Use the list of words above to complete the following sentences.

1. The girl kept a toad, a lizard, and a gerbil in her private _____.
2. The Golden Pavilion is a famous _____ in Japan.
3. The beautiful dress is made of a _____ fabric.
4. The girl's shoes were a _____ size.
5. A great _____ uses only the finest ingredients to prepare delicious food.
6. We hired an experienced _____ to drive the car.
7. The leader picked the best marchers to form an _____ drill team.

Name _____

Match the letter beside each definition to the correct word.

1. _____ **comrade**   a. small house with one story

2. _____ **clan**   b. a good friend

3. _____ **solo**   c. hardly enough, small amount

4. _____ **scant**   d. head cook

5. _____ **petite**   e. a group of travelers or vehicles traveling together

6. _____ **brocade**   f. group of related families bearing the same name, and following the same leader

7. _____ **pagoda**   g. anything done alone

8. _____ **menagerie** h. temple of several stories, found in Far East

9. _____ **bungalow**   i. small and trim

10. _____ **elite**   j. a person hired to drive a car

11. _____ **caravan**   k. a rich cloth with a raised design

12. _____ **chauffeur** l. a collection of animals; place where animals are kept

13. _____ **chef**   m. group or part of a group selected as the best, most powerful

Choose five words from the list above. Use each one in a sentence.

1. _____

_____

2. _____

_____

3. _____

_____

4. _____

_____

5. _____

Name _____

Many English words come from the Greek language.

comedy	cone	biology	theater
rhythm	star	drama	music
grammar	geometry	theory	meter

Use the words in the word box to complete the crossword puzzle.

Across

3. a unit of length
4. the study of points, lines, surfaces, and figures
8. the study of living things
9. a building where plays are performed
10. a story performed on a stage
11. a repetition of sounds or movements

Down

1. a pointed object with a round base
2. a bright heavenly body
4. a system of rules for using words
5. a pleasing combination of sounds
6. an idea that explains why something happens
7. an amusing story

Name _____

Read the words in the word box and pick out the ones with the same Greek or Latin base word. Write them in the correct group below. Then use a dictionary to write the meanings of the words.

cycle	section	bicycle	telephone	extract
tractor	phonics	dissect	dynamite	intersect
dynasty	cyclone	dynamic	symphony	traction

1. *sectus* (Latin)—to cut

    a. _____

    b. _____

    c. _____

2. *cyclus* (Latin)—circle

    a. _____

    b. _____

    c. _____

3. *phone* (Greek)—sound

    a. _____

    b. _____

    c. _____

4. *tractus* (Latin)—to pull

    a. _____

    b. _____

    c. _____

5. *dynamis* (Greek)—power

    a. _____

    b. _____

    c. _____

Name _____

The words in the word box are imported words. Write each word beside its description.

key	gopher	woodchuck	coleslaw
skunk	prairie	moose	boss
poodle	sleigh	porcupine	cockroach
squash	chowder	cookie	

1. This word came from the Dutch word **koolsla** meaning *cabbage salad.* ___ ___ ___ ___ ___ ___ ___ ___

2. This word came from the French word **porc d'espine** meaning *spine-porker.* ___ ___ ___ ___ ___ ___ ___ ___ ___

3. This word, meaning a *low island*, came from the Spanish word **cayo**. ___ ___ ___

4. This word was shortened from the Native American word **askutusquash**. ___ ___ ___ ___ ___ ___

5. This word came from a French word that means *big meadow.* ___ ___ ___ ___ ___ ___ ___

6. This word came from the Native American word **moosu** meaning *stripper of bark*. ___ ___ ___ ___ ___

7. This word came from the Dutch word **koekje** meaning *cake*. ___ ___ ___ ___ ___ ___

8. This word came from the German word **pudelhund** meaning *splash-dog.* ___ ___ ___ ___ ___ ___

9. This word came from the Native American word **segankw**. ___ ___ ___ ___ ___

10. This word came from the Dutch word **slee**. ___ ___ ___ ___ ___ ___

11. This word came from the Native American word **otchuck**. ___ ___ ___ ___ ___ ___ ___ ___ ___

12. This word came from the French word **chaudiere** meaning *big pot.* ___ ___ ___ ___ ___ ___ ___

13. This word came from the Spanish word **cucaracha**. ___ ___ ___ ___ ___ ___ ___ ___ ___

14. This word's actual origin is unknown, but it may have come from the French word **gaufre**. ___ ___ ___ ___ ___ ___

15. This word came from the Dutch word **baas** meaning *master.* ___ ___ ___ ___

Name _____

Write the imported food word next to its description.

pizza	ketchup	bread	mushroom	spaghetti	boysenberry
cabbage	shrimp	pumpkin	lettuce	omelette	vegetable
broccoli	salami	radish	chowder	chocolate	Brazil nut

1. From a Latin word meaning head ___ ___ _b_ ___ ___ ___ ___

2. Named for Rudolph Boysen, an American horticulturist who developed this plant ___ ___ ___ ___ ___ ___ ___ ___ ___ ___ _y_ ___

3. From a German word meaning to shrivel up ___ _h_ ___ ___ ___ ___

4. From an Italian word meaning *small nail* ___ ___ ___ _c_ ___ ___ ___ ___

5. From a French word meaning *moss* ___ ___ _s_ ___ ___ ___ ___ ___

6. From a Greek word meaning to *ripen in the sun* ___ ___ ___ _p_ ___ ___ ___

7. From two Maya words meaning *sour water* ___ ___ ___ ___ _c_ ___ ___ ___ ___

8. Named for the South American country in which it grows
___ ___ ___ ___ ___ ___ _n_ ___ ___

9. From a Latin word meaning root ___ ___ ___ ___ _s_ ___

10. From a French word meaning *thin blade of a sword* ___ ___ ___ ___ ___ _t_ ___ ___

11. From a Latin word meaning *milk-giving plant* ___ ___ ___ ___ ___ _c_ ___

12. From an Italian word meaning *cord* or *string* ___ ___ ___ _g_ ___ ___ ___ ___ ___

13. From a Chinese word that referred to a spicy fish sauce ___ ___ ___ _c_ ___ ___ ___

14. From an Old English word meaning *piece* or *fragment* ___ _r_ ___ ___ ___

15. From a French word meaning *kettle* ___ _h_ ___ ___ ___ ___ ___

16. From a Latin word meaning to *rouse, excite* ___ ___ _g_ ___ ___ ___ ___ ___ ___

17. From a Latin word meaning to *pound* ___ ___ ___ _z_ ___

18. From an Italian word meaning to *salt* ___ ___ ___ _a_ ___ ___

Name _____

An **abbreviation** is the **shortened form** of a word.

Write an abbreviation for each day of the week and month.

HAPPY DAYS ARE HERE AGAIN!

A. Sunday _____

B. Monday _____

C. Tuesday _____

D. Wednesday _____

E. Thursday _____

F. Friday _____

G. Saturday _____

Unscramble the abbreviations for the days of the week.

t   s   a   n   u   s   o   n   m   e   d   w

___ ___ ___   ___ ___ ___   ___ ___ ___   ___ ___ ___

s   u   t   e   r   i   f   r   s   t   u   h

___ ___ ___ ___   ___ ___ ___   ___ ___ ___ ___ ___

Name _____

Write the whole word next to its abbreviation.

1. Blvd. _____   9. Dec. _____

2. Sr. _____   10. Etc. _____

3. Jan. _____   11. Tues. _____

4. Mr. _____   12. Dr. _____

5. Thurs. _____   13. St. _____

6. Sept. _____   14. Mt. _____

7. Rte. _____   15. Jr. _____

8. Feb. _____   16. Ave. _____

Senior	Route	December	September
Street	Mister	Tuesday	Boulevard
Junior	Doctor	February	Thursday
Mountain	Avenue	January	Et cetera

Name _____

Write the whole word next to its abbreviation.

1. ave. _____

2. Dr. _____

3. apt. _____

4. C.O.D. _____

5. secy. _____

6. dept. _____

7. elem. _____

8. govt. _____

9. m.p.h. _____

10. hwy. _____

11. cm _____

12. F _____

13. bldg. _____

14. I.Q. _____

15. mt. _____

16. Jr. _____

17. doz. _____

18. p.s. _____

19. Mr. _____

20. lb. _____

21. p.o. _____

22. rd. _____

23. Wed. _____

24. Gov. _____

25. St. _____

26. C _____

road   mountain   government   highway   building   pound

miles per hour   department   Celsius   postscript   centimeter
secretary   Mister   Doctor   Street   post office   avenue
Governor   dozen   Wednesday   apartment   elementary
Junior   fahrenheit   Intelligence Quotient   Cash On Delivery

Name _____

Replace each abbreviation with its meaning.

secretary	elementary
appointment	apartment
governor	building
dozen	street

1. I go to Robert Louis Stevenson Elem. _____

2. Can you come over to my apt. after school? _____

3. I heard your St. is under construction right now. _____

4. My brother lives in bldg. 3 on campus. _____

5. This year I was elected secy. of the class. _____

6. I have a dentist appt. after school today. _____

7. The Gov. will visit our school as part of
   his campaign.   _____

8. Please pick up a doz. donuts for the troop meeting. _____

Name _____

A **compound word** is made up of **two words** that can stand alone. Match two words from the word box to make a compound word. Write the words on the lines.

light	basket	lip	dog
house	candle	foot	boat
broom	moon	stick	ball

1. _____   8. _____

2. _____   9. _____

3. _____   10. _____

4. _____   11. _____

5. _____   12. _____

6. _____   13. _____

7. _____   14. _____

Name _____

Match two words from the word box to make a compound word. Write six sentences using the compound words you made.

fire	gold	rain	star
coat	man	bird	bath
snow	bed	fish	room

1. _____

2. _____

3. _____

4. _____

5. _____

6. _____

Name _____

Match two words from the word box to make a compound word. Write a definition for six of the compound words you made.

night	down	bed	hand
town	hill	boy	up
back	stairs	time	paper

1. _____

2. _____

3. _____

4. _____

5. _____

6. _____

Name _____

Write a sentence using each compound word from the word box.

classmate	tiptoe
starfish	somebody
woodland	airport
popcorn	hardware

1. _____

2. _____

3. _____

4. _____

5. _____

6. _____

7. _____

8. _____

Name _____

Replace the <u>underlined</u> words with a compound word.

1. Jenny wears her hair in a <u>tail</u>
   <u>that looks like that of a pony</u>. _____

2. Remember to follow the speed limit
   on the <u>way where you are free to drive</u>
   <u>without having to stop for lights</u>. _____

3. Danny won several <u>fish that</u>
   <u>are gold colored</u> at the carnival._____

4. Can you hand me a <u>pin with which</u>
   <u>I can clip clothes to a line</u>? _____

5. Did you have <u>meal made of</u>
   <u>oats</u> this morning at breakfast?_____

6. Yin got a new <u>watch to wear on his wrist</u>
   at the beginning of the school year._____

7. We're playing a <u>game involving</u>
   <u>bases and a ball</u> after school today._____

8. Twist the <u>knob on the door</u> carefully. _____

PAGE 4

Classification   Name _____

Classification means to put objects together in **groups**.
Rhinoceros, human, and **chimpanzee** are all **mammals**.

Write each animal name in the correct group.

Birds
ostrich	bald eagle
pelican	owl

Amphibians
bullfrog	salamander
toad	newt

Reptiles
cobra	gecko
Gila monster	chameleon

Fish
salmon	sailfish
tuna	rainbow trout

Mammals
killer whale	wolf
aardvark	gorilla

cobra	aardvark	tuna	rainbow trout	gecko
salmon	killer whale	bullfrog	newt	owl
ostrich	toad	sailfish	salamander	wolf
pelican	bald eagle	Gila monster	chameleon	gorilla

PAGE 5

THIS CARNIVORE IS QUITE CRANKY!

Circle the word in each group that is unlike the rest.

1. carnivore — herbivore — omnivore — (nocturnal)
2. quartz — (nylon) — iron pyrite — turquoise
3. ice — steam — water — (pitcher)
4. (launch pad) — comet — planet — asteroid
5. gecko — chameleon — (squirrel) — Gila monster
6. grasshopper — termite — firefly — (anteater)
7. circulatory — digestive — (metric) — nervous
8. pine — sunflower — (sunlight) — cabbage
9. hurricane — tornado — (space) — earthquake
10. (apple) — wheat — soybean — oats
11. (whale) — shark — tarpon — salmon
12. steel — aluminum — (plastic) — copper
13. (microphone) — microscope — telescope — binoculars

PAGE 6

An **analogy** uses **word relationships** to compare one group to another group:
Swim is to water as ski is to snow.

Read each sentence carefully. Write the word that completes the sentence on the line.

1. Cut is to scissors as slice is to **knife**.
   bread
   knife

2. Boat is to lake as ship is to **ocean**.
   ocean
   sail

3. Eye is to see as ear is to **hear**.
   hear
   ring

4. Cup is to drink as plate is to **eat**.
   wash
   eat

5. Ink is to pen as paint is to **brush**.
   picture
   brush

6. Thermometer is to temperature as clock is to **time**.
   time
   hour

7. Chick is to hen as kitten is to **cat**.
   cat
   cute

8. Toe is to foot as finger is to **hand**.
   nail
   hand

PAGE 7

Cross out the word that does not belong. Then write a word from the word box that does belong. Write a title above each list.

flute	Seattle	division	daffodil	motorcycle	noun

1. **flowers**
   sunflower — rose
   daisy — tulip
   ~~lettuce~~ — carnation
   daffodil

2. **math**
   fraction — ~~sentence~~
   equals — addition
   subtraction — multiplication
   division

3. **instruments**
   trombone — drums
   ~~cherry~~ — piano
   guitar — violin
   flute

4. **grammar**
   comma — period
   colon — pronoun
   verb — ~~seven~~
   noun

5. **vehicles**
   scooter — ~~car~~
   bike — ~~toaster~~
   skateboard — truck
   motorcycle

6. **cities**
   New York — Dallas
   Paris — London
   ~~marker~~ — Chicago
   Seattle

PAGE 8

Complete each analogy with a word from the word box.

footprint	run
condensation	light
darkness	bacteria
stomach	chameleon

A WORM IS TO A FISH AS A CHEESEBURGER IS TO A FIFTH GRADER!

HEY DUDE— WHERE'S THE FRIES?

1. Warm-blooded is to cold-blooded as a bear is to a __chameleon__.
2. Gravity is to weightlessness as light is to __darkness__.
3. Ear is to sound as eye is to __light__.
4. Bird is to fly as cheetah is to __run__.
5. Dinosaur is to fossil as shoe is to __footprint__.
6. Telescope is to planets as microscope is to __bacteria__.
7. Lifeless is to living as evaporation is to __condensation__.
8. Blood vessel is to heart as intestine is to __stomach__.

PAGE 9

Complete each analogy.

1. **Lead** is to **pencil** as **ink** is to __pen__.
2. **Foot** is to **sock** as **head** is to __hat__.
3. **Scoop** is to **ice cream** as **slice** is to __cake or bread__.
4. **Hot** is to **summer** as **cold** is to __winter__.
5. **Rain** is to **wet** as **sunshine** is to __dry__.
6. **Smile** is to **happy** as **cry** is to __sad__.
7. **Dark** is to **black** as **light** is to __white__.
8. **Earring** is to **ear** as **necklace** is to __neck__.
9. **Calf** is to **cow** as **kitten** is to __cat__.
10. **Airplane** is to **fly** as **car** is to __drive__.
11. **Snake** is to **slither** as **ant** is to __crawl__.
12. **Cheetah** is to **fast** as **snail** is to __slow__.

PAGE 10

Synonyms are words that mean the **same** thing. **Cute** and **adorable** are **synonyms**.

Circle the synonyms for the first word in each row.

1. fast (quick) hard (swift) (speedy) small
2. bright (dazzling) dull (glittering) (sparkling)
3. friend stranger (companion) (chum) (pal) (buddy)
4. scary scream (frightening) rough (terrifying)
5. throw (fling) carry (hurl) (toss) catch

Look at the picture below. Using the words you circled write a list of synonyms to describe each picture.

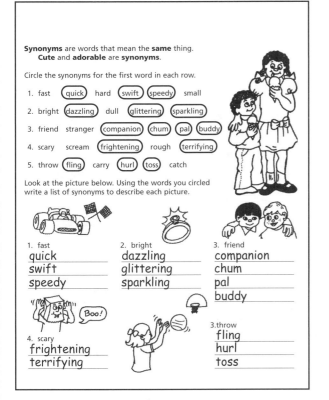

1. fast
quick
swift
speedy

2. bright
dazzling
glittering
sparkling

3. friend
companion
chum
pal
buddy

4. scary
frightening
terrifying

3. throw
fling
hurl
toss

PAGE 11

Choose the word from the word box that could replace the **boldfaced** word in each sentence. Write the word on the line.

fortunate	discovered	grimy	ancient
sizzling	entire	select	chuckle

1. The dinosaur bones were **old**.

ancient

2. We were **lucky** that it didn't rain.

fortunate

3. After playing football, my clothes were **dirty**.

grimy

4. That joke made me **laugh**.

chuckle

5. I rode my bike the **whole** way home.

entire

6. I had to **choose** a book for my report

select

7. It was a **hot** day in the desert.

sizzling

8. I **found** the missing puzzle piece on the floor.

discovered

PAGE 12

Use the words from the word box to write a synonym for each underlined word.

Dear Pen Pal,

I was glad **happy**

to get **receive**

your letter. Soccer is my

favorite sport too **also**.

And I have three brothers who

always bother **tease**

me, too! Seattle sounds like a great **enjoyable** place to live, but I

wouldn't enjoy **like** all the rain. It's always sunny and hot

scorching in Houston. My friends and I like viewing

watching movies and going out for ice cream afterwards. I like

chocolate best **most**.

enjoyable
receive
also
scorching
most
friend
tease
like
happy
watching

Your Pal **friend** ,

_____

PAGE 13

Circle the two words in each row that are synonyms.

1. (mistake) (error) repair
2. (rich) money (wealthy)
3. (frighten) (startle) secret
4. song (noisy) (loud)
5. (imitate) (copy) return
6. (hasty) funny (speedy)
7. (cheap) expensive (inexpensive)
8. break (repair) (fix)
9. (travel) (vacation) work
10. (gift) (present) watch
11. (friend) enemy (pal)
12. (watch) (see) mean

PAGE 14

Answer the clues using words from the word box to complete the puzzle.

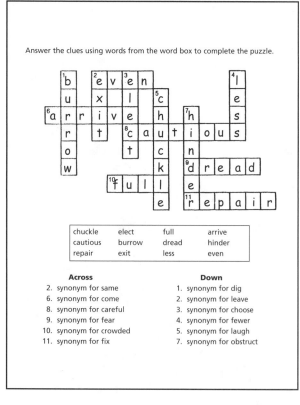

chuckle	elect	full	arrive
cautious	burrow	dread	hinder
repair	exit	less	even

Across
2. synonym for same
6. synonym for come
8. synonym for careful
9. synonym for fear
10. synonym for crowded
11. synonym for fix

Down
1. synonym for dig
2. synonym for leave
3. synonym for choose
4. synonym for fewer
5. synonym for laugh
7. synonym for obstruct

PAGE 15

An **antonym** is a word that means the **opposite**.

Answer the clues using words from the word box to complete the puzzle.

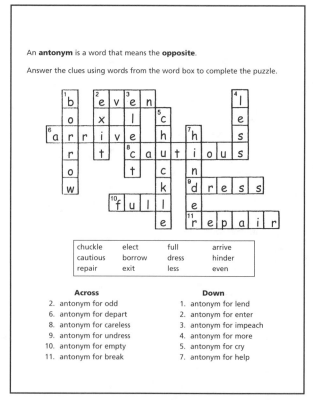

chuckle	elect	full	arrive
cautious	borrow	dress	hinder
repair	exit	less	even

Across
2. antonym for odd
6. antonym for depart
8. antonym for careless
9. antonym for undress
10. antonym for empty
11. antonym for break

Down
1. antonym for lend
2. antonym for enter
3. antonym for impeach
4. antonym for more
5. antonym for cry
7. antonym for help

PAGE 16

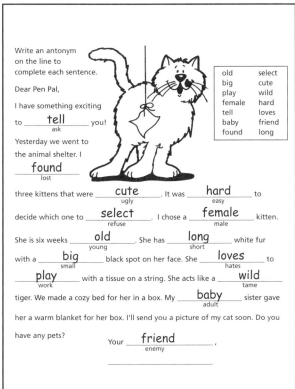

Write an antonym on the line to complete each sentence.

old	select
big	cute
play	wild
female	hard
tell	loves
baby	friend
found	long

Dear Pen Pal,

I have something exciting to ___**tell**___ you!

<small>ask</small>

Yesterday we went to the animal shelter. I ___**found**___

<small>lost</small>

three kittens that were ___**cute**___ . It was ___**hard**___ to

<small>ugly</small>   <small>easy</small>

decide which one to ___**select**___ . I chose a ___**female**___ kitten.

<small>refuse</small>   <small>male</small>

She is six weeks ___**old**___ . She has ___**long**___ white fur

<small>young</small>   <small>short</small>

with a ___**big**___ black spot on her face. She ___**loves**___ to

<small>small</small>   <small>hates</small>

___**play**___ with a tissue on a string. She acts like a ___**wild**___

<small>work</small>   <small>tame</small>

tiger. We made a cozy bed for her in a box. My ___**baby**___ sister gave

<small>adult</small>

her a warm blanket for her box. I'll send you a picture of my cat soon. Do you

have any pets?   Your ___**friend**___ ,

                     <small>enemy</small>

PAGE 17

Circle the two words in each row that have opposite meanings.

1. return   (break)   (fix)
2. (rich)   (poor)   wealth
3. (light)   sun   (dark)
4. (loud)   nosy   (quiet)
5. (borrow)   (lend)   reduce
6. haste   (slow)   (speedy)
7. (cheap)   (expensive)   silly
8. watch   (break)   (repair)
9. travel   (play)   (work)
10. (lost)   (found)   cook
11. write   (buy)   (sell)
12. (kind)   friendly   (mean)

PAGE 18

Write an antonym for each word.

1. son   daughter
2. lost   found
3. chilly   warm
4. whole   part
5. speak   listen
6. sent   receive
7. bare   covered
8. won   lost
9. male   female
10. high   low
11. sell   buy
12. girl   boy
13. dark   light
14. empty   full
15. inside   outside

PAGE 19

Whoops!

Each sentence below was meant to say the opposite. Circle the incorrect word in each sentence. Choose a word from the word box to replace it. Rewrite each sentence using the new word.

| sad | after | hard | odd | apart | borrow |

1. I chipped a tooth on the (soft) candy.

   I chipped a tooth on the hard candy.

2. Three and five are (even) numbers.

   Three and five are odd numbers.

3. My puzzle pieces fell (together).

   My puzzle pieces fell apart.

4. June comes (before) May.

   June comes after May.

5. I was (happy) when my friend moved.

   I was sad when my friend moved.

6. May I (lend) your eraser?

   May I borrow your eraser?

PAGE 20

Homonyms are words that **sound similar** but **mean different things** and are sometimes **spelled differently**.

Write the missing word in each sentence.

way weigh	1. How much does the puppy **weigh**?
	2. Which **way** do you walk home?
not knot	3. I am **not** going to be late.
	4. Can you untie the **knot**?
our hour	5. That is **our** house.
	6. We will be home in an **hour**.
eight ate	7. He **ate** two hot dogs.
	8. There are **eight** people here.
here hear	9. Did you **hear** the news?
	10. Put the letter in **here**.
too two	11. Can you come **too**?
	12. She has **two** sisters.
bee be	13. I was stung by a **bee**.
	14. Will you **be** home at three?
pair pear	15. Pick a **pear** from the tree.
	16. I need a new **pair** of shoes.

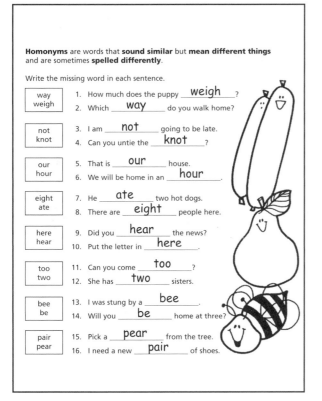

PAGE 21

Choose the correct word to complete each sentence. Then write the meaning of the word you chose on the line below the sentence.

desert — very dry land

dessert — after-meal treat

1. Dad made us pudding for a special **dessert**.

2. We drove across miles of sandy **desert**.

lose — misplace

loose — not tight

3. My brother's sweater was too **loose**.

4. The money is in my pocket so I won't **lose** it.

single — only, one

signal — warning sign

1. The **single** letter in the mailbox was for me.

2. The red light was a **signal** to stop.

PAGE 22

Read the list below. Two different meanings are given for each word.

iris	1) a type of flower	2) colored part of the
eye		
perch	1) a type of fish	2) a bird's resting place
bill	1) notice of money owed	2) a bird's beak
trunk	1) storage area of car	2) an elephant's nose
ruler	1) a person who governs	2) a tool for measuring
spring	1) to leap forward	2) a coil of wire
log	1) a daily record	2) section of a tree

Decide which meaning the **boldfaced** word has in each sentence below. Then write the meaning on the line.

1. I had enough money to pay the **bill**.
   notice of money owed
2. We put the suitcases in the **trunk**.
   storage area of car
3. You'll need a **ruler** to check the length.
   a tool for measuring
4. Keep a **log** of your progress.
   a daily record
5. A purple **iris** is growing in the garden.
   a type of flower
6. The clock needs a new **spring**.
   a coil of wire
7. Put another **log** on the fire.
   section of a tree
8. I think I caught a **perch**.
   a type of fish
9. She was the nation's **ruler**.
   a person who governs
10. A duck has an orange **bill**.
    a bird's beak

PAGE 23

Read the pairs of homonyms in the word box. Read the story below and circle each incorrect word. Then rewrite the story using the correct words.

know	for	threw	sale	flour	rolls	isle	pairs
no	four	through	sail	flower	roles	aisle	pears
by	one	cereal	beats	weekly	steak	There	so
buy	won	serial	beets	weekly	stake	Their	sew

In the Bag

It was time ~~four~~ the ~~weakly~~ grocery shopping. Dad takes me because I ~~no~~ a good ~~by~~ when I see ~~won~~. We walked ~~threw~~ every ~~isle~~ looking for what was on ~~sail~~. ~~Their~~ were specials on ~~stake~~, ~~serial~~, ~~pairs~~, ~~flower~~, ~~beats~~, and ~~roles~~, ~~sew~~ we stocked up.

In the Bag

It was time for the weekly grocery shopping. Dad takes me because I know a good buy when I see one. We walked through every aisle looking for what was on sale. There were specials on steak, cereal, pears, flour, beets, and rolls, so we stocked up!

PAGE 24

Rewrite each sentence using the correct homonym.

1. My Ant Betty always bakes the Thanksgiving turkey.
   My Aunt Betty always bakes the Thanksgiving turkey.

2. Tim caught the fowl ball and threw it back to the pitcher.
   Tim caught the foul ball and threw it back to the pitcher.

3. Mom used the smelly chemical when ceiling the basement walls.
   Mom used the smelly chemical when sealing the basement walls.

4. That banned played at the school picnic.
   That band played at the school picnic.

5. You are such a deer to help me carry in the groceries.
   You are such a dear to help me carry in the groceries.

6. The weatherman says this reign will last a few more days.
   The weatherman says this rain will last a few more days.

PAGE 25

Read the pairs of words in the word box. Then read the story below. Circle the incorrect words. Then rewrite the story using the right words.

| road | waist | lone | weight | by |
| rode | waste | loan | wait | buy |

Land of His Own

The cowboy (road) his horse into town. He didn't (waist) any time getting there. He went to the bank to get a (lone). He had to (weigh) awhile. But soon he had money to (by) land of his own!

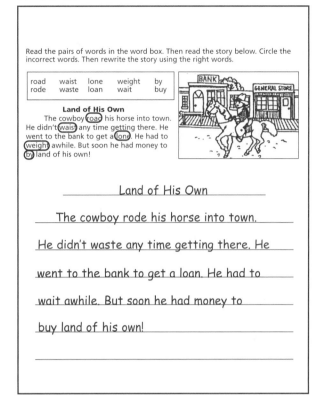

Land of His Own

The cowboy rode his horse into town.

He didn't waste any time getting there. He

went to the bank to get a loan. He had to

wait awhile. But soon he had money to

buy land of his own!

PAGE 26

Context clues are clues you can find in a sentence to help you figure out **what a word means**.

Write the letter of the best meaning of the underlined word on the line before each sentence.

1. **B** The gardener planted the flowers in a bed that would get lots of sunshine.

2. **C** The bed of coals glowed orange and yellow in the darkness. It was perfect for roasting marshmallows.

3. **A** Terri jumped into bed and pulled the covers up to her chin. She curled up and began reading her book.

   A. a piece of furniture used for sleeping   B. a plot of ground prepared for plants   C. a flat layer

4. **C** Nancy rounded third base and ran for home plate.

5. **A** Maclin took the photographic plate to the printer so the newspaper could be published.

6. **B** George put salad and a burger on his plate.

   A. a smooth, flat, thin piece of material   B. a dish to eat from   C. a square bag to mark a place

7. **C** Please match the sentence with the best answer.

8. **A** The class was watching the tennis match.

9. **B** Gail lit the match. She used it to light the birthday candles.

   A. a contest   B. a small stick with a flammable material on the end used to start a fire   C. put together into a pair

PAGE 27

Choose the best meaning for the underlined word as used in the sentence. Write a checkmark on the line next to your choice.

1. As Meg walked out of the room, she turned the switch to off and the light went out.
   ___ A. to change from one thing to another
   ✓ B. something used to turn off and on lights
   ___ C. a slender, flexible rod or twig

2. Dad told the children that they should have minded him. If they had, the bikes would not have been stolen.
   ___ A. something you think with
   ___ B. to dig minerals out of the earth
   ✓ C. to follow someone's directions

3. Jean carefully removed the wax from the mold. Each candle was shaped like a star.
   ✓ A. a form for making something into a certain shape
   ___ B. a fuzzy growth
   ___ C. the surface of the earth

4. Alex moved the dash up and down. It became harder to move as the cream turned into butter.
   ___ A. a short line
   ___ B. to run very quickly
   ✓ C. the handle of the butter churn

5. Mom put a little pat of butter on the side of the plate.
   ___ A. to gently pet or tap
   ___ B. someone's name
   ✓ C. a small individual portion

6. Choose two underlined words and write them on the lines below. Then use them in sentences. Use different definitions than the ones used in the sentences above.

   Answers will vary.

PAGE 28

Circle the word(s) that is closest in meaning to the underlined word.

1. Cheryl's umbrella hat was so peculiar looking that everyone in the entire park stared over at it!

    bright   large   (unusual)

2. Sandra insisted on being prompt for the concert because she didn't want to miss a single minute of the performance.

    (on time)   late   ready to laugh

3. David's pet rabbit is so brilliant that it even asks to help make the dinner salad!

    available   rich   (incredibly smart)

4. The kids on Amanda's new street were so considerate that they introduced themselves on the day she moved in.

    rude   fortunate   (polite)

5. Mark wanted to catch the same kind of butterfly that Jeff did so badly that he asked everyone if there were any more in the vicinity.

    house   (area)   shopping mall

6. The watermelon from Curt's garden was so enormous that he had to use a wheelbarrow to carry it into the house!

    (gigantic)   colorful   funny-shaped

7. Michele caught a glimpse of the new swimming pool as she rode her bike past the gate.

    taste   understanding   (quick look)

8. Eva's poodle clenched the stick in its teeth.

    (grabbed tightly)   chewed   scratched

9. Because there was such a variety of kites to choose from, Jolie had no idea what to buy!

    (large selection)   mess   small amount

10. Cyndi was very apprehensive about buying the iguana until she found out that iguanas are herbivorous!

    happy   excited   (unsure)

11. After Peter finished making the bread, he realized he had left out one of the most important ingredients — the yeast!

    cooking utensil   color   (part of the mixture)

12. Monica was amazed at the perfectly shaped hexagons that the bees had made in their hive.

    flower bouquets   (6-sided polygons)   honey treats

PAGE 29

Read each sentence carefully. Write a short definition for each underlined word.

1. A child fidgeted uncomfortably on the bench.

    _____

2. After losing her wallet, Mattie was on the brink of tears.

    _____

3. In the smoky, smog-filled neighborhood, the jogger yearned for clean air.

    _____

4. Mike became more upbeat after finishing his homework and started working on his model airplane.

    _____

5. The friends became somber when Renee announced that her family was moving to Wisconsin.

    _____

6. Penny felt sluggish after helping her mom in the garden all day.

    _____

Answers will vary.

PAGE 30

Circle the word which best completes each sentence.

1. Kevin slowly picked up his _____ to play the Chopin nocturne.

    toothpick   (clarinet)   piano

2. With fearful trepidation, he lifted the mouthpiece to his _____.

    ears   chest   (lips)

3. Out of the bell of his reed instrument came a _____ squawk.

    (horrendous)   peaceful   loving

4. Mrs. Dee Canon abruptly lowered her _____.

    button   shoe   (baton)

5. "Who so shockingly _____ in a goose from his or her barnyard?" she asked.

    (brought)   danced   cooked

6. Feeling so _____ he could have hidden under his chair, Kevin raised his hand.

    daring   (awful)   sleepy

7. Forty-two pairs of eyes turned to stare at the _____-red face of this would-be Benny Goodman.

    potato   (beet)   celery

8. Mrs. Canon, noting Kevin's chagrin, calmly regained the attention of her _____.

    ears   clarinet   (class)

9. "Who can tell me the last time they didn't make a rude sound with a _____ instrument?" she began.

    scientific   (musical)   electronic

10. "Oh," entered Sean _____, "I remember that four months ago Sunday I didn't make a mistake."

    (understandingly)   madly   cryptically

11. "And _____ was that?" asked Mrs. Canon, amused by Sean's wisdom.

    who   what   (why)

12. "Well, you know, we didn't get our instruments until the next _____," replied Sean.

    Christmas   pizza   (Monday)

13. Mrs. Canon looked at every band member who _____ and nodded their heads.

    hollered   (smiled)   marched

14. "Kevin," she said softly, "you're doing fine. My goodness! I _____ on my trumpet for two years solid. Just ask my mother."

    (squealed)   stepped   played

15. Kevin almost smiled, though he kept his head _____.

    nodding   askew   (lowered)

16. Raising her baton once more, Mrs. Canon returned to the nocturne, and the _____ played on.

    game   (band)   toys

PAGE 31

Read the passage carefully. Find and write a **boldfaced** word from the passage for each description below.

Computer Data

Computers may seem "smart" but they cannot think. The only thing they can do is follow a set of instructions called a **program** which must be written by a person. The computer **hardware** (machinery) and **software** (programs) work together.

For the computer to work, a person must enter **data**, or information, into the computer. This is called **input**. New data is entered by typing on a **keyboard** that has letters and symbols like a typewriter. Data may be stored on a **disk** which is used to record and save information.

Next, the computer "reads" the data and follows the instructions of the program. The program may tell it to organize the data, compare it to other data, or store it for later use. This is called data **processing**.

When the processing is complete, the computer can display the results either on the screen or printed on paper as a **printout**.

1. _disk_ used to save and record information
2. _processing_ organizing, comparing, or storing data
3. _printout_ results printed on paper
4. _program_ set of instructions for a computer
5. _hardware_ computer machinery
6. _input_ entering data
7. _software_ computer programs
8. _keyboard_ where data is entered

PAGE 32

Concept words are words that have to do with a certain **topic** or **idea**. Complete the puzzle on page 33 using the clues and the word box below.

HMMM...
PUZZLING!

Across

3. An _____ is the darkening of one heavenly body by another.

5. The gas that we need in order to live is called _____.

6. An _____ eats both plants and animals.

10. A _____ eats only plants.

11. The _____ contains all the colors of the rainbow and white light.

Down

1. _____ is the process by which plants use carbon dioxide and sunlight to make food.

2. An _____ studies the different celestial bodies.

4. A frozen mass of dust and ice with a long tail that travels around the sun is called a _____.

7. The air that surrounds the earth is called our _____.

8. A _____ is two or more atoms joined together.

9. A _____ eats only meat.

photosynthesis	carnivore	eclipse
spectrum	herbivore	oxygen
atmosphere	omnivore	comet
astronomer	molecule	

PAGE 33

PAGE 34

Many interesting words are based on Greek and Roman mythology.

Read the names and descriptions of the gods and goddesses below. Then use this information to help you match the letter beside the English word to the correct definition. Write the letters in the blanks.

Sol—Roman sun god
Luna—Roman goddess of the moon
Mars—Roman god of war
Faunus—Roman god of animals
Ceres—Roman goddess of agriculture, especially grains
Hygeia—Greek goddess of health

	Definition	*English word*
1. __e__	animals of a particular region	a. martial
2. __a__	relating to military or war	b. hygiene
3. __f__	any food made from grain, such as wheat, oats, or rice	c. solar
4. __b__	practice of good health habits	d. lunar
5. __c__	having to do with the sun	e. fauna
6. __d__	relating to the moon	f. cereal

Write one of the six English words above to complete each sentence below.

7. The nurses went to the villages to teach better __hygiene__.

8. The __solar__ panels collect energy from the sun.

9. Many young people learn karate, one of the __martial__ arts.

10. The wildlife expert was making a study of the park's __fauna__.

11. The student ate a breakfast of milk and __cereal__.

12. Tonight, there will be a __lunar__ eclipse.

PAGE 35

Write the state for each capital. Use a map to help you.

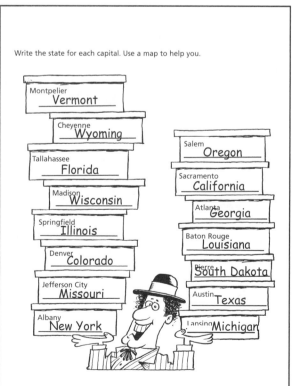

Montpelier __Vermont__

Cheyenne __Wyoming__

Salem __Oregon__

Tallahassee __Florida__

Sacramento __California__

Madison __Wisconsin__

Atlanta __Georgia__

Springfield __Illinois__

Baton Rouge __Louisiana__

Denver __Colorado__

Pierre __South Dakota__

Jefferson City __Missouri__

Austin __Texas__

Albany __New York__

Lansing __Michigan__

PAGE 36

Complete each sentence with a word from the word box. Then complete the puzzle.

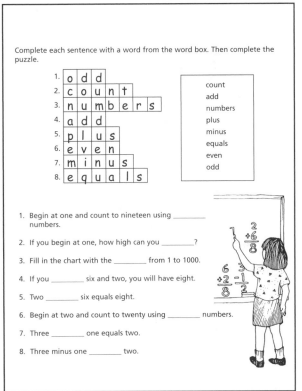

1. o d d
2. c o u n t
3. n u m b e r s
4. a d d
5. p l u s
6. e v e n
7. m i n u s
8. e q u a l s

count
add
numbers
plus
minus
equals
even
odd

1. Begin at one and count to nineteen using _____ numbers.

2. If you begin at one, how high can you _____?

3. Fill in the chart with the _____ from 1 to 1000.

4. If you _____ six and two, you will have eight.

5. Two _____ six equals eight.

6. Begin at two and count to twenty using _____ numbers.

7. Three _____ one equals two.

8. Three minus one _____ two.

PAGE 37

Read the passage carefully.

Many children like to take part in games because they enjoy the **action** of a sport.

In tennis class, they learn to **volley** the ball, hitting it back quickly before it touches the ground. They **warm up** before the games to get ready for a **match**. Their teachers, or **coaches**, encourage them to do their best. In tennis, **deuce** means the score is tied at 40, so the players have to work hard to score the next two points to get ahead. When they become good players, people may come to watch them play.

Write the **boldfaced** words next to their meanings in the tennis balls below.

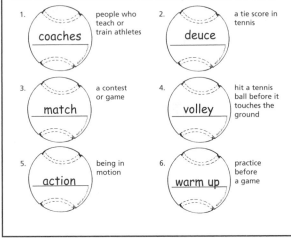

1. coaches — people who teach or train athletes

2. deuce — a tie score in tennis

3. match — a contest or game

4. volley — hit a tennis ball before it touches the ground

5. action — being in motion

6. warm up — practice before a game

PAGE 38

A **sensory word** describes something you **smell, touch, taste, see,** or **hear**. Write a word from the word box that describes the phrase.

pop
growl
buzz
bang
splash
squeak
clop
cock-a-doodle-doo

1. a horse's hooves on the pavement __clop__

2. popcorn in the microwave __pop__

3. a mouse behind the stove __squeak__

4. a kid in a puddle of water __splash__

5. a rooster at dawn __cock-a-doodle-doo__

6. a bee around a flower __buzz__

7. a door slamming __bang__

8. a dog showing its teeth __growl__

PAGE 39

Match the sense with the sensory word.

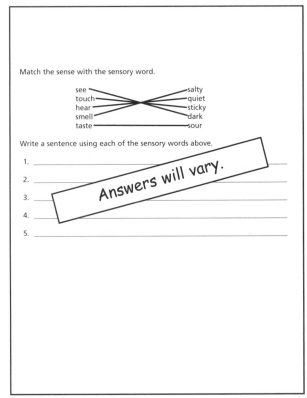

see — salty
touch — quiet
hear — sticky
smell — dark
taste — sour

Write a sentence using each of the sensory words above.

1. _____
2. _____
3. _____
4. _____
5. _____

Answers will vary.

PAGE 40

Rewrite each sentence using at least two sensory words.

1. Can you hear that?

   _____

2. Look at that!

   _____

3. This is my project.

   _____

4. This b_____

   _____

5. My friend is nice.

   _____

Answers will vary.

PAGE 41

Read the cues in the word box. Write a paragraph answering each cue. Use sensory words to develop your ideas.

| My favorite . . . | I am . . . | I ate . . . | I play . . . |
| My friend . . . | I feel . . . | I study . . . | I like . . . |

Answers will vary.

PAGE 42

Onomatopoeia is a word that **sounds like** the sound it describes. Read each onomatopoeia word. Write a sentence describing the cause of the noise.

1. slop

2. murmur

3. fizz

4. knock

5. whine

6. thunk

Answers will vary.

PAGE 43

A **plural** is **more than one** of a person, place, or thing. Remember
   Change **y** to **i** and add **es**
   Words that end in **sh, ch, x,** or **z** add **es**
   Change **f** to **v** and add **es**

Change each word to the plural form. Write the word on the line.

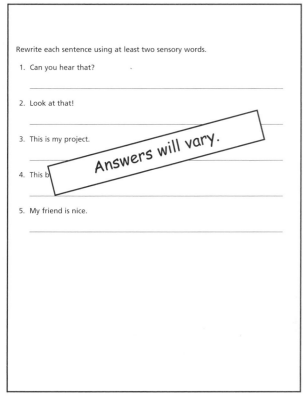

1. The _____leaves_____ are pretty colors.
   leaf
2. We picked _____berries_____ in the woods.
   berry
3. We saw a movie about _____wolves_____.
   wolf
4. The _____calves_____ are in the barn.
   calf
5. There are two _____libraries_____ in the city.
   library
6. Dad built _____shelves_____ in the garage.
   shelf
7. It costs a dollar to ride the _____ponies_____.
   pony
8. The story is about seven tiny _____elves_____.
   elf
9. _____Fireflies_____ are fun to watch at night.
   Firefly
10. Mother planted _____lilies_____ in the yard.
    lily
11. The mother lion has three _____babies_____.
    baby
12. The police caught the _____thieves_____.
    thief

PAGE 44

THESE WORDS HAVE GOT ME ALL SHOOK UP!

THANKYOUVERYMUCH.

Make the following words plural.

1. cranberry cranberries
2. bunny bunnies
3. calf calves
4. church churches
5. rainbow rainbows
6. watch watches
7. life lives
8. hobby hobbies
9. notch notches
10. vicinity vicinities
11. psalm psalms
12. index indexes or indices
13. half halves
14. suffix suffixes
15. symphony symphonies

PAGE 45

Make the following words plural by adding **s** or **es**.

1. ostrich ostriches
2. buffalo buffaloes
3. camper campers
4. balloon balloons
5. toothbrush toothbrushes
6. birch birches
7. caterpillar caterpillars
8. lunch lunches
9. tomato tomatoes
10. paragraph paragraphs
11. skateboard skateboards
12. volcano volcanoes
13. potato potatoes
14. class classes
15. sandbox sandboxes
16. notebook notebooks
17. fossil fossils

BUFFALO? AIN'T THAT NEAR ROCHESTER?

PAGE 46

Write the plural of each word on the line. Then write the plural in the correct box puzzle.

1. match matches
2. city cities
3. school schools
4. foot feet
5. body bodies
6. church churches
7. man men
8. radio radios
9. calf calves
10. penny pennies
11. child children
12. piano pianos
13. woman women
14. story stories
15. sandwich sandwiches
16. mouse mice

pennies calves
radios stories
matches sandwiches
schools women
children mice
churches pianos cities
men bodies feet

PAGE 47

A **suffix** is a word part added to the **end of a word** to change its meaning.

-ist
A noun-forming suffix, -ist means a person who makes, does, or practices.

-ly
An adverb- or adjective-forming suffix, -ly means when, how, like, or in the manner of.

-less
An adjective-forming suffix, -less means without or lacking.

-fy
A verb-forming suffix, -fy means to make or cause to be or become.

-ness
A noun-forming suffix, -ness means state or quality of being.

-ize
A verb-forming suffix, -ize means to cause to be or to become.

From the following list, select the correct word to complete each sentence. Write the word on the line.

vaporize   naturalist   harshly   purify   pitiless   correctness

1. Before drinking river water you should purify it because it may be polluted.
2. A person who practices the study of nature is a naturalist.
3. The pitiless football coach made the team run an extra mile.
4. Check your spelling for correctness when using new words.
5. The angry man spoke harshly to the telephone operator.
6. High temperatures will make water vaporize.

Use the suffixes in the word box to make new words that answer each phrase. Write the word on the line.

7. An adjective meaning without power. powerless
8. An adverb that tells how a brave person acts. bravely
9. A verb meaning to make simple. simplify
10. A noun meaning a person who makes works of art. artist
11. A verb meaning to form crystals. crystallize
12. A noun meaning the state of being dark. darkness

PAGE 48

Use the word box to fill in the blanks with words containing suffixes. Put each boxed letter in the matching numbered blank below to find out the state you might visit to get something necessary for school.

invitation	penniless	wonderful	hopeless
careful	noisy	collection	peaceful
addition	followed	winning	

1. h o **p** e l e s s
2. **a** d d i t i o n
3. f o **l l** o w e d
4. w i n n i **n** g
5. w o **n** d e r f u l
6. c **a** r e f u l
7. i n **v** i t a t i o n
8. c o l l e **c** t i o n
9. **n** o i s y
10. p e a c e **f** u l
11. p e n n **i** l e s s

p e n n s y l v a n i a
1 10 5 8 11 3   7 2 9 4 6

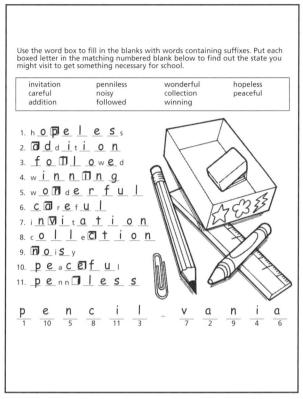

PAGE 49

The suffix **able** means *capable of*. For example, a wire that is **bendable** can bend.

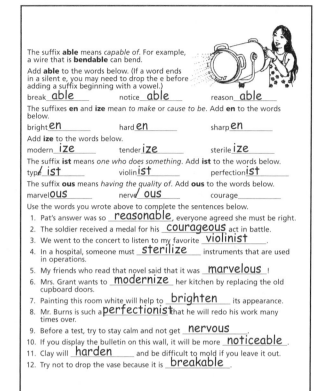

Add **able** to the words below. (If a word ends in a silent e, you may need to drop the e before adding a suffix beginning with a vowel.)

break **able**   notice **able**   reason **able**

The suffixes **en** and **ize** mean *to make* or *cause to be*. Add **en** to the words below.

bright **en**   hard **en**   sharp **en**

Add **ize** to the words below.

modern **ize**   tender **ize**   sterile **ize**

The suffix **ist** means *one who does something*. Add **ist** to the words below.

typ~~e~~ **ist**   violin **ist**   perfection **ist**

The suffix **ous** means *having the quality of*. Add **ous** to the words below.

marvel **ous**   nerv~~e~~ **ous**   courage

Use the words you wrote above to complete the sentences below.

1. Pat's answer was so **reasonable**, everyone agreed she must be right.
2. The soldier received a medal for his **courageous** act in battle.
3. We went to the concert to listen to my favorite **violinist**.
4. In a hospital, someone must **sterilize** instruments that are used in operations.
5. My friends who read that novel said that it was **marvelous**!
6. Mrs. Grant wants to **modernize** her kitchen by replacing the old cupboard doors.
7. Painting this room white will help to **brighten** its appearance.
8. Mr. Burns is such a **perfectionist** that he will redo his work many times over.
9. Before a test, try to stay calm and not get **nervous**.
10. If you display the bulletin on this wall, it will be more **noticeable**.
11. Clay will **harden** and be difficult to mold if you leave it out.
12. Try not to drop the vase because it is **breakable**.

PAGE 50

Read the passage carefully.

"The treasure must be in here!" yelled Brad. He and his sister Lauren stood outside the **entrance** of a cave. As Brad took a step towards the **darkness**, Lauren touched his arm.

"Let's rest a bit," said Lauren, still **breathless** from running. "Besides, it might be **dangerous** in there."

Brad held up a tattered notebook that had *Abigail* etched faintly on its cover. "This diary we found says Abigail hid a treasure in here," he said. "I want to find it before anyone else does." Brad turned and stepped inside the cave with **determination**. Lauren sighed and **reluctantly** followed her brother.

Brad waved his flashlight impatiently around the cave. Moments later he cried, "I see something!" Brad stooped down and started digging in the earth with a rock. Lauren came to help. Soon the two uncovered a small **wooden** box. Brad's hands shook with **excitement**. He took the box outside and opened it. Brad and Lauren gasped and looked at the contents in **astonishment**. Inside were letters addressed to Abigail.

"Nothing but letters!" moaned Brad with **disappointment**. "There's no treasure here at all." He sank to the ground feeling tired and a bit **foolish**.

Lauren stood with a **thoughtful** look on her face. "If it's any **consolation**," she said slowly, "we did find Abigail's treasure." Lauren fingered the letters **gently** and continued, "These letters were written by someone whose **friendship** Abigail felt very strongly about. She probably put the letters in the cave for safekeeping."

Write the **boldfaced** words beside their meanings below. Circle the suffix in each word.

1. place of entry entr**ance**
2. out of breath breath**less**
3. state of being excited excite**men**t
4. having little or no light dark**ness**
5. great surprise astonish**men**t
6. unwise fool**ish**
7. deep in thought thought**ful**
8. state of being friends friend**ship**
9. with unwillingness reluctant**ly**
10. act of being comforted consola**tion**
11. feeling let down disappoint**men**t
12. quality of being firm determina**tion**
13. in a gentle manner gent**ly**
14. made of wood wood**en**
15. involving something that can cause harm danger**ous**

PAGE 51

Read the passage carefully.

Alina and Melissa arrived home after playing at their friend's house. It was only seven o'clock, but **darkness** had already fallen. The porch lights were on, offering a **cheery** welcome to the two sisters.

"It was fun playing Megan's new video game," said Alina as she and Melissa walked up the driveway.

"It sure was," agreed Melissa. Suddenly she stopped and touched her sister's arm. "What's that?" she whispered in a **fearful** voice.

Alina followed her sister's gaze. There by the steps leading to their front door was a plump, furry creature with a **bushy** tail and **beady** eyes. At first the girls thought it was a large cat, but they realized they were wrong when they noticed the animal's thin snout.

"It's an opossum!" gasped Alina in **amazement**. "Don't move. It might be **dangerous**."

The girls stared at the animal, making no noise or **movement**. How they wished they could be inside their safe, **comfortable** home! Alina and Melissa yearned to take the few quick steps needed to reach the front door and **freedom**, but they knew a move like that could **frighten** the opossum. So the girls waited, each hopeful that their unexpected **visitor** would get tired and leave. If they were not so worried, their situation might have appeared **comical** to them.

After what seemed hours, the opossum turned and scurried into the blackness. "I'm glad he's gone," said Alina with a sigh of relief. "For awhile, I was **doubtful** he would ever leave!"

"Me, too," said Melissa. "Come on, let's go inside before he decides to visit us again!"

Write the **boldfaced** words beside their meanings below. Circle the suffix in each word.

1. able to cause harm danger**ous**
2. showing fear fear**ful**
3. bright and pleasant cheer**y**
4. thick and spreading bush**y**
5. act of moving move**men**t
6. a guest visit**or**
7. state of comfort comfort**able**
8. small, round, and shiny bead**y**
9. without light dark**ness**
10. cause to be afraid fright**en**
11. great surprise amaze**men**t
12. funny comic**al**
13. not sure doubt**ful**
14. state of being free free**dom**

PAGE 52

The suffixes **ion** and **ity** mean the **state or quality of**. Add the suffix **ion** or **ity** to each word below.

1. the state of being protected   protection
2. the quality of being scarce   scarcity
3. the quality of being necessary   necessity
4. the state of combining   combination
5. the state of colliding   collision
6. the state of being divided   division
7. the state of being permitted   permission
8. the quality of being active   activity
9. the state of being received   recession
10. the state of being directed   direction

PAGE 53

A **prefix** is a part **added to the beginning** of a word to change its meaning. The prefix **un** means **not** and the prefix **re** means **again**. Add the correct prefix to each word in the word box. Write the new words in the correct column.

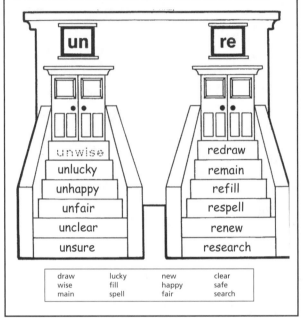

un	re
unwise	redraw
unlucky	remain
unhappy	refill
unfair	respell
unclear	renew
unsure	research

draw	lucky	new	clear
wise	fill	happy	safe
main	spell	fair	search

PAGE 54

Read each definition. Complete each sentence using a word with the prefix **un** or **re**.

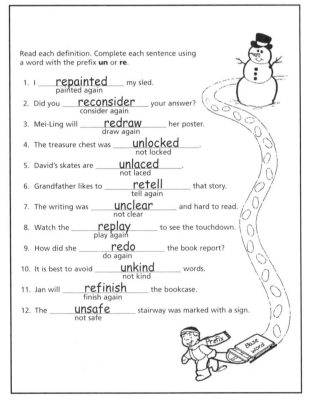

1. I **repainted** my sled.
   painted again
2. Did you **reconsider** your answer?
   consider again
3. Mei-Ling will **redraw** her poster.
   draw again
4. The treasure chest was **unlocked**.
   not locked
5. David's skates are **unlaced**.
   not laced
6. Grandfather likes to **retell** that story.
   tell again
7. The writing was **unclear** and hard to read.
   not clear
8. Watch the **replay** to see the touchdown.
   play again
9. How did she **redo** the book report?
   do again
10. It is best to avoid **unkind** words.
    not kind
11. Jan will **refinish** the bookcase.
    finish again
12. The **unsafe** stairway was marked with a sign.
    not safe

PAGE 55

The prefix **mis** means **wrongly** and the prefix **non** means **not**. Add the correct prefix to each word in the word box. Write the new words in the correct column.

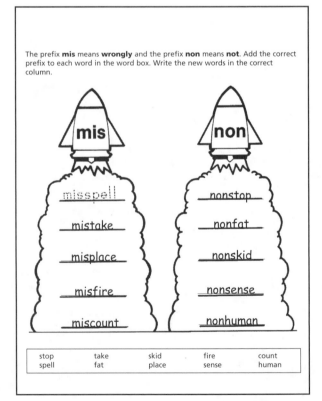

mis	non
misspell	nonstop
mistake	nonfat
misplace	nonskid
misfire	nonsense
miscount	nonhuman

stop	take	skid	fire	count
spell	fat	place	sense	human

PAGE 56

The prefix **mis** means **wrongly** and the prefix **pre** means **before**.
Add the prefix to each word. Write the new word and then write its meaning.

Base Word	Prefix	New Word	Meaning
1. cook	pre	precook	cook beforehand
2. spell	mis	misspell	spell wrong
3. view	pre	preview	look at beforehand
4. school	pre	preschool	before kindergarten
5. pay	pre	prepay	pay ahead of time
6. place	mis	misplace	lose
7. use	mis	misuse	not use properly
8. treat	mis	mistreat	not treat properly

PAGE 57

The prefixes **im** and **dis** mean **not**. Add the correct prefix to each word in the word box. Write the new words in the correct column.

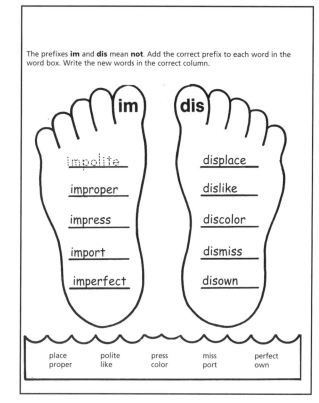

im
impolite
improper
impress
import
imperfect

dis
displace
dislike
discolor
dismiss
disown

| place | polite | press | miss | perfect |
| proper | like | color | port | own |

PAGE 58

Circle each word in the puzzle with a prefix. Write the words below. Circle the prefix.

```
I B E L O W U D I R Z H D
N O N F A T N E M P S R B
S O E M P J C B P R U W I
I M X Z O O L U G E B A C
D I S L I K E G I S W B Y
E S T N W B A R M O A O C
S T R A V P R E P A Y A L
F A R E L I V E O K C R E
T K L A S J S N R J Y D M
T E L E G R A M T C H O S
```

1. inside
2. mistake
3. unclear
4. debug
5. import
6. presoak
7. subway
8. aboard
9. bicycle
10. below
11. nonfat
12. dislike
13. relive
14. prepay
15. telegram

PAGE 59

Some words have Latin prefixes. Use the meanings of the Latin prefixes in the word box to help you write the English word for each definition below.

| com | = together | semi | = half; partly | dis | = opposite |
| pre | = before | re | = back; again | sub | = below |

1. a half circle — semicircle
2. below zero — subzero
3. heat again — reheat
4. view before — review
5. opposite of agree — disagree
6. write again — rewrite
7. gain back — regain
8. partial darkness — semidark
9. press together — compress
10. opposite of honest — dishonest
11. appear again — reappear
12. opposite of respect — disrespect

PAGE 60

A **root** or **base word** is the word that is left after you **take off a prefix or suffix.**

	auto	self
autobiography	the story of a person's life written by that person	
autograph	a person's signature or handwriting	
automatic	having a self-acting or self-regulating mechanism; done without thought or conscious effort	
automobile	a passenger vehicle with its own engine	
autonomous	self-governing	

Divide the following words into parts so the root is separate.

1. automobile — auto / mobile
2. autobiography — auto / biography
3. automatic — auto / matic
4. autograph — auto / graph
5. autonomous — auto / nomous

Complete each sentence using a word from the word box.

1. The writer finished the _autobiography_ about her life.
2. Sally got an _automatic_ camera for her birthday.
3. Jose was excited when he got the celebrity's _autograph_.
4. The people who lived on the island did not wish to be governed by a mother country any longer. They wanted to be _autonomous_.

PAGE 61

	multi	many
multicolored	having many colors	
multimedia	combining more than two artistic techniques or means of communication or expression, such as acting, lighting effects, and music	
multimillionaire	a person who has at least two million dollars	
multiple	having many parts or elements	
multitude	a large number of persons or things	

Unscramble the word and write the definition.

Example: limptule   multiple   having many parts or elements

1. rollutimedoc — multicolored — having many colors
2. lemonlimitailiur — multimillionaire — a person who has at least two million dollars
3. demiltutu — multitude — a large number of persons or things
4. immediatul — multimedia — combining many art techniques

Complete each sentence using a word from the word box.

1. The unhappy result of John's skiing accident was a _multiple_ fracture of the arm.
2. A kaleidoscope is constructed with _multicolored_ glass.
3. The rock concert with television screens and a light show was a _multimedia_ event.
4. A _multimillionaire_ donated money for the starving children.
5. The _multitude_ of people followed the celebrity into the theater.

PAGE 62

	pre	before
preamble	a statement that introduces a formal document, explaining its purpose	
precede	to come or go before in rank, time, or order	
prehistoric	of the period before written history	
preoccupied	wholly occupied or absorbed in one's thoughts; absentminded	
preschool	school before kindergarten; nursery school	
prevent	to take action before an event to stop the event from happening	

Write a short definition for each word.

Example: prehistoric of the period before written history.

1. precede
2. precedent
3. preoccupation
4. prevention
5. preventable

Answers will vary.

Complete each sentence using a word from the word box.

1. The four-year-old child will attend a _preschool_ class.
2. The dinosaurs lived during _prehistoric_ times.
3. The teacher said we had to memorize the _preamble_ to the United States Constitution.
4. Roger couldn't enjoy the movie because he was _preoccupied_ about the test the next day.
5. Seventh grade _precedes_ (s) eighth grade.

PAGE 63

	bi, di	two
biceps	any muscle having two points of origin	
bilingual	able to use two languages equally well	
biped	a two-footed animal	
bisect	divide into two (usually equal) parts	
dichromatic	having two colors	
dilemma	a situation requiring a choice between two equal alternatives	
diploma	a certificate awarded when a student has successfully completed a particular course of study	
dipterous	having two wings	

Complete each sentence using a word from the word box.

1. A fly is a _dipterous_ insect.
2. Lorenzo was taking a course in weight training, and would proudly flex his _biceps_ when anyone asked how he was progressing.
3. Charlotte faced the _dilemma_ of whether to go to the movie with her friends or take the baby-sitting job.
4. Silvia is _bilingual_ because she speaks Spanish at home and English at school.
5. The geometry teacher told the students to _bisect_ the circle.

Write a word with the prefix **bi** to complete each phrase.

1. *Annual* means once a year. _Biannual_ means twice a year.
2. A *biennium* is a two-year period. _Biennial_ means once every two years.
3. *Centum* is the Latin word for one hundred. _Bicentennial_ means once every two hundred years.
4. A _bimonthly_ event happens twice a month.
5. A _biweekly_ event happens twice a week.

PAGE 64

Root and Base Words

Name _____

	ben, bene	good, well

benediction	a blessing
benefactor	a person who gives help or support, especially financial aid
beneficial	having a good or helpful effect
beneficiary	a person who receives a benefit or advantage, such as an inheritance
benevolent	doing good things; being good-hearted, kind
benign	gentle and kind; not threatening life

Fill in each blank with a word from the word box.
1. The musician needed a _benefactor_ to support him financially.
2. The priest said the _benediction_ after the mass.
3. It is _beneficial_ to study vocabulary before taking a standardized test.
4. The _beneficiary_ of his life insurance policy would receive $25,000.
5. My grandmother was very relieved when the tests showed that the tumor was _benign_.

Circle each word below in which **ben** or **bene** is used as a prefix meaning good, well.

(bene)ath   Benelux
(Bene)dict   (benigh)ted
(bene)factor   benignant
benefit   benumb

List five things that are beneficial to your health.

1. _____
3. _____

Answers will vary.

PAGE 65

	cred	to believe

accredit	to give credit for; to authorize or recognize officially
credence	acceptance or belief
credential	letter or document that proves or affirms a person's identity or right to hold a certain position
credo	a set of beliefs or opinions
credulous	inclined to believe anything, often without sufficient proof
discredit	to reject as untrue; to cast doubt on; to disgrace
incredible	unbelievable

Fill in each blank with a word from the word box.

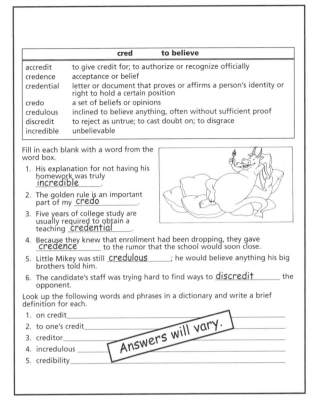

1. His explanation for not having his homework was truly _incredible_.
2. The golden rule is an important part of my _credo_.
3. Five years of college study are usually required to obtain a teaching _credential_.
4. Because they knew that enrollment had been dropping, they gave _credence_ to the rumor that the school would soon close.
5. Little Mikey was still _credulous_; he would believe anything his big brothers told him.
6. The candidate's staff was trying hard to find ways to _discredit_ the opponent.

Look up the following words and phrases in a dictionary and write a brief definition for each.

1. on credit _____
2. to one's credit _____
3. creditor _____
4. incredulous _____
5. credibility _____

Answers will vary.

PAGE 66

	hydr, hydro	water

dehydrate	to lose or remove water
hydrant	a large, upright pipe connected to a water main
hydraulics	being operated by or using a liquid
hydrocarbon	any of a large class of organic compounds that contain only carbon and hydrogen
hydroelectric	of or relating to electricity produced by the energy of flowing water, such as that from a dam
hydrophobia	an abnormal fear of water; rabies
hydroplane	a light, fast boat designed to skim along the surface of water; a seaplane

Fill in each blank with a word from the word box.
1. We crossed the English Channel in a _hydroplane_.
2. To make raisins, you _dehydrate_ grapes.
3. Hoover Dam is an important source of _hydroelectric_ power.
4. On extremely hot days, the mayor orders all _hydrants_(s) to be opened so that people can cool off in the water.
5. Because it causes an inability to swallow liquids, rabies is also known as _hydrophobia_.

Look up these hydro words in the dictionary. Write their meanings.

1. hydra _____
2. hydrogen _____
3. hydrolysis _____
4. hydroponics _____
5. hydrothermal _____

Answers will vary.

PAGE 67

Imported words are English words that **come from other languages**, such as German, French, or Latin.
Look up the following words in a dictionary. Write the definition in the blank beside each word.

1. **chef** (from French) _____
2. **chauffeur** (from French) _____
3. **petite** (from French) _____
4. **brocade** (from Spanish) _____
5. **pagoda** (from Portuguese) _____
6. **elite** (from French) _____
7. **menagerie** (from French) _____

Answers will vary.

Use the list of words above to complete the following sentences.
1. The girl kept a toad, a lizard, and a gerbil in her private _menagerie_.
2. The Golden Pavilion is a famous _pagoda_ in Japan.
3. The beautiful dress is made of a _brocade_ fabric.
4. The girl's shoes were a _petite_ size.
5. A great _chef_ uses only the finest ingredients to prepare delicious food.
6. We hired an experienced _chauffeur_ to drive the car.
7. The leader picked the best marchers to form an _elite_ drill team.

PAGE 68

Match the letter beside each definition to the correct word.

1. **b** comrade   a. small house with one story
2. **f** clan   b. a good friend
3. **g** solo   c. hardly enough, small amount
4. **c** scant   d. head cook
5. **i** petite   e. a group of travelers or vehicles traveling together
6. **k** brocade   f. group of related families bearing the same name, and following the same leader
7. **h** pagoda   g. anything done alone
8. **l** menagerie   h. temple of several stories, found in Far East
9. **a** bungalow   i. small and trim
10. **m** elite   j. a person hired to drive a car
11. **e** caravan   k. a rich cloth with a raised design
12. **j** chauffeur   l. a collection of animals; place where animals are kept
13. **d** chef   m. group or part of a group selected as the best, most powerful

Choose five words from the list above. Use each one in a sentence.

1. _____
2. _____
3. _____ *Answers will vary.*
4. _____
5. _____

PAGE 69

Many English words come from the Greek language.

comedy	cone	biology	theater
rhythm	star	drama	music
grammar	geometry	theory	meter

Use the words in the word box to complete the crossword puzzle.

Across
3. a unit of length
4. the study of points, lines, surfaces, and figures
8. the study of living things
9. a building where plays are performed
10. a story performed on a stage
11. a repetition of sounds or movements

Down
1. a pointed object with a round base
2. a bright heavenly body
4. a system of rules for using words
5. a pleasing combination of sounds
6. an idea that explains why something happens
7. an amusing story

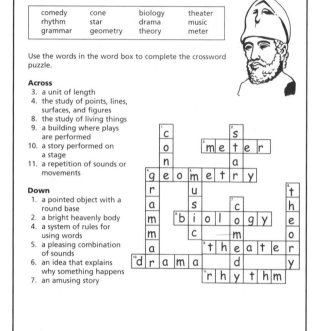

Crossword answers: meter, geometry, biology, theater, drama, rhythm; comedy, star, grammar, music, cone, theory

PAGE 70

Read the words in the word box and pick out the ones with the same Greek or Latin base word. Write them in the correct group below. Then use a dictionary to write the meanings of the words.

cycle	section	bicycle	telephone	extract
tractor	phonics	dissect	dynamite	intersect
dynasty	cyclone	dynamic	symphony	traction

1. *sectus* (Latin)—to cut
   a. section
   b. dissect
   c. intersect
2. *cyclus* (Latin)—circle
   a. cycle
   b. cyclone
   c. bicycle
3. *phone* (Greek)—sound
   a. phonics
   b. telephone
   c. symphony
4. *tractus* (Latin)—to pull
   a. tractor
   b. extract
   c. traction
5. *dynamis* (Greek)—power
   a. dynasty
   b. dynamic
   c. dynamite

PAGE 71

The words in the word box are imported words. Write each word beside its description.

key	gopher	woodchuck	coleslaw
skunk	prairie	moose	boss
poodle	sleigh	porcupine	cockroach
squash	chowder	cookie	

1. This word came from the Dutch word **koolsla** meaning *cabbage salad*. coleslaw
2. This word came from the French word **porc d'espine** meaning *spine-porker*. porcupine
3. This word, meaning a *low island*, came from the Spanish word **cayo**. key
4. This word was shortened from the Native American word **askutusquash**. squash
5. This word came from a French word that means *big meadow*. prairie
6. This word came from the Native American word **moosu** meaning *stripper of bark*. moose
7. This word came from the Dutch word **koekje** meaning *cake*. cookie
8. This word came from the German word **pudelhund** meaning *splash-dog*. poodle
9. This word came from the Native American word **segankw**. skunk
10. This word came from the Dutch word **slee**. sleigh
11. This word came from the Native American word **otchuck**. woodchuck
12. This word came from the French word **chaudiere** meaning *big pot*. chowder
13. This word came from the Spanish word **cucaracha**. cockroach
14. This word's actual origin is unknown, but it may have come from the French word **gaufre**. gopher
15. This word came from the Dutch word **baas** meaning *master*. boss

PAGE 72

Write the imported food word next to its description.

pizza	ketchup	bread	mushroom	spaghetti	boysenberry
cabbage	shrimp	pumpkin	lettuce	omelette	vegetable
broccoli	salami	radish	chowder	chocolate	Brazil nut

1. From a Latin word meaning head c a b b a g e
2. Named for Rudolph Boysen, an American horticulturist who developed this plant b o y s e n b e r r y
3. From a German word meaning to shrivel up s h r i m p
4. From an Italian word meaning *small nail* b r o c c o l i
5. From a French word meaning *moss* m u s h r o o m
6. From a Greek word meaning to *ripen in the sun* p u m p k i n
7. From two Maya words meaning *sour water* c h o c o l a t e
8. Named for the South American country in which it grows B r a z i l n u t
9. From a Latin word meaning root r a d i s h
10. From a French word meaning *thin blade of a sword* o m e l e t t e
11. From a Latin word meaning *milk-giving plant* l e t t u c e
12. From an Italian word meaning *cord* or *string* s p a g h e t t i
13. From a Chinese word that referred to a spicy fish sauce k e t c h u p
14. From an Old English word meaning *piece* or *fragment* b r e a d
15. From a French word meaning *kettle* c h o w d e r
16. From a Latin word meaning to *rouse, excite* v e g e t a b l e
17. From a Latin word meaning to *pound* p i z z a
18. From an Italian word meaning to *salt* s a l a m i

PAGE 73

An **abbreviation** is the **shortened form** of a word.
Write an abbreviation for each day of the week and month.

HAPPY DAYS ARE HERE AGAIN!

A. Sunday Sun.
B. Monday Mon.
C. Tuesday Tues.
D. Wednesday Wed.
E. Thursday Thurs.
F. Friday Fri.
G. Saturday Sat.

Unscramble the abbreviations for the days of the week.

t s a   n u s   o n m   e d w
S a t   S u n   M o n   W e d

s u t e   r i f   r s t u h
T u e s   F r i   T h u r s

PAGE 74

Write the whole word next to its abbreviation.

1. Blvd. Boulevard
2. Sr. Senior
3. Jan. January
4. Mr. Mister
5. Thurs. Thursday
6. Sept. September
7. Rte. Route
8. Feb. February

9. Dec. December
10. Etc. Et cetera
11. Tues. Tuesday
12. Dr. Doctor
13. St. Street
14. Mt. Mountain
15. Jr. Junior
16. Ave. Avenue

Senior	Route	December	September
Street	Mister	Tuesday	Boulevard
Junior	Doctor	February	Thursday
Mountain	Avenue	January	Et cetera

PAGE 75

Write the whole word next to its abbreviation.

1. ave. avenue
2. Dr. Doctor
3. apt. apartment
4. C.O.D. Cash On Delivery
5. secy. secretary
6. dept. department
7. elem. elementary
8. govt. government
9. m.p.h. miles per hour
10. hwy. highway
11. cm centimeter
12. F Fahrenheit
13. bldg. building

14. I.Q. Intelligence Quotient
15. mt. mountain
16. Jr. Junior
17. doz. dozen
18. p.s. post script
19. Mr. Mister
20. lb. pound
21. p.o. post office
22. rd. road
23. Wed. Wednesday
24. Gov. Governor
25. St. Street
26. C Celsius

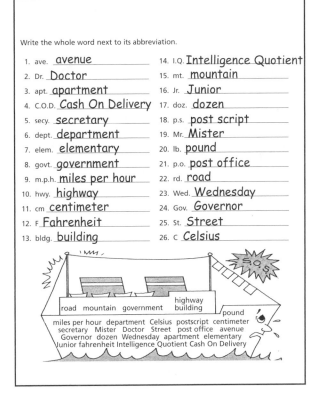

road mountain government highway building pound
miles per hour department Celsius postscript centimeter
secretary Mister Doctor Street post office avenue
Governor dozen Wednesday apartment elementary
Junior fahrenheit Intelligence Quotient Cash On Delivery

PAGE 76

Replace each abbreviation with its meaning.

secretary	elementary
appointment	apartment
governor	building
dozen	street

1. I go to Robert Louis Stevenson Elem. **Elementary**

2. Can you come over to my apt. after school? **apartment**

3. I heard your St. is under construction right now. **street**

4. My brother lives in bldg. 3 on campus. **building**

5. This year I was elected secy. of the class. **secretary**

6. I have a dentist appt. after school today. **appointment**

7. The Gov. will visit our school as part of his campaign. **Governor**

8. Please pick up a doz. donuts for the troop meeting. **dozen**

PAGE 77

A **compound word** is made up of **two words** that can stand alone. Match two words from the word box to make a compound word. Write the words on the lines.

light	basket	lip	dog
house	candle	foot	boat
broom	moon	stick	ball

1. lighthouse
2. houseboat
3. doghouse
4. basketball
5. football
6. stickball
7. lipstick
8. moonlight
9. broomstick
10. candlelight
11. boathouse
12. housebroom
13. houselight
14. broomball

PAGE 78

Match two words from the word box to make a compound word. Write six sentences using the compound words you made.

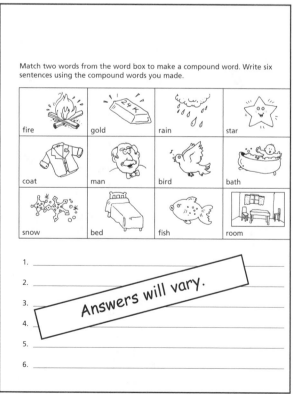

fire	gold	rain	star
coat	man	bird	bath
snow	bed	fish	room

1. _____
2. _____
3. _____ Answers will vary.
4. _____
5. _____
6. _____

PAGE 79

Match two words from the word box to make a compound word. Write a definition for six of the compound words you made.

night	down	bed	hand
town	hill	boy	up
back	stairs	time	paper

1. _____
2. _____
3. _____ Answers will vary.
4. _____
5. _____
6. _____

PAGE 80

Write a sentence using each compound word from the word box.

classmate	tiptoe
starfish	somebody
woodland	airport
popcorn	hardware

1. _____
2. _____
3. _____
4. _____
5. _____
6. _____
7. _____
8. _____

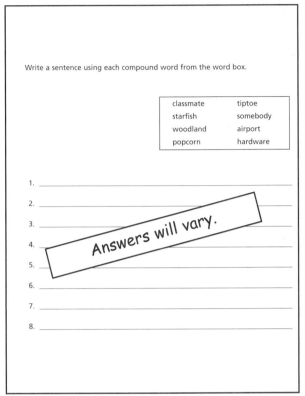
Answers will vary.

PAGE 81

Replace the underlined words with a compound word.

1. Jenny wears her hair in a <u>tail</u> <u>that looks like that of a pony</u>. __ponytail__

2. Remember to follow the speed limit on the <u>way where you are free to drive without having to stop for lights</u>. __freeway__

3. Danny won several <u>fish that are gold colored</u> at the carnival. __goldfish__

4. Can you hand me a <u>pin with which I can clip clothes to a line</u>? __clothespin__

5. Did you have <u>meal made of oats</u> this morning at breakfast? __oatmeal__

6. Yin got a new <u>watch to wear on his wrist</u> at the beginning of the school year. __wristwatch__

7. We're playing a <u>game involving bases and a ball</u> after school today. __baseball game__

8. Twist the <u>knob on the door</u> carefully. __doorknob__

Name _____

Test-taking Practice is designed to prepare you to use the Vocabulary Skills you've been practicing in the first part of this book on a standardized test.

The first part of the Test-taking Practice is just for Vocabulary Skills. You'll answer questions that test your knowledge of synonyms, Antonyms, Homonyms, and Context Clues.

The second part of the Test-taking Practice is Reading Comprehension. On these pages, you will read a passage and then answer questions about it. The better your understanding of Vocabulary Skills, such as Context Clues, Concept Words, and Root and Base Words, the better you will do on Reading Comprehension, which indirectly tests these skills.

How to Use Test-Taking Practice

Getting Started:
- Read the directions carefully.
- Do the sample items.

Practice:
- Complete the Practice items.
- Continue working until you reach a Stop sign at the bottom of the page.

Name _____

Sometime during school you may take a standardized achievement test. These tests check to see what you and the rest of your class have learned. they can help you see what your strengths and weaknesses are.

Taking a test can be stressful, but it doesn't have to be! The key is to prepare yourself, whether you are taking an achievement test or a weekly quiz. Here are some tips that can help you prepare for and do your best on any kind of test.

Before the test:
- Find a comfortable, quiet spot to study that is free of distractions.
- Get organized before you start to study: collect all the books, papers, notes, and pencils or pens you will need before you sit down.
- Study a little bit at a time, no more than 30 minutes a day. If you can, choose the same time each day to study in your quiet place. This is good practice for sitting and concentrating for the actual test.
- Give yourself frequent 5-minute breaks if you plan to study for longer than a half hour. Stand up, stretch out, and get a drink or snack (nothing too messy!)
- Try making a study sheet with all the information you think will be on the test. Have a parent, brother, sister, or friend quiz you by asking questions from the sheet.

On the day of the test:
- Get a good night's sleep before the test.
- Plan to eat a light breakfast and lunch so that you won't get drowsy during the test. Too much food can make you sleepy.
- Wear comfortable clothes that won't distract you during the test. If you have long hair, plan to pull it back away from your face so it won't distract you.
- Don't worry if you are a little nervous when you take a test. This is a natural feeling and may even help you stay alert.
- Take advantage of any breaks you have. Stand up and stretch, and get a drink of water or visit the bathroom if you have the time.

Name _____

During the test:

Be careful

- Listen carefully to all the directions before you begin.

- Read all directions carefully.

- Sometimes the letters for the answer choices change for each question. Make sure the space you fill in matches the answer you think is correct.

- Read the question and all the answer choices. Once you have decided on the correct answer, ask yourself: "Does this really answer the question?"

Manage your time wisely

- Take the time to understand each question before you answer.

- Eliminate the answer choices that don't make sense.

- Try out answer choices in the question to see if they make sense.

- Skim through written passages and then read the questions. Refer back to the story to answer the questions. You don't have to reread the passage for each question.

- Look for key words in the question and the answer choices. They will help you find the correct answer.

- Sometimes the correct answer is not given. Mark "none" if this is the case.

- Skip difficult questions. Circle them and come back to them when you are finished with the easier questions.

- If there is still time when you have finished, go through the test again and check your answers.

Be confident

- Stay with your first answer. Change it only if you are certain another choice is better.

- Don't worry if you don't know an answer. Take your best guess if you are unsure of the answer, then move on to the next question.

- Be certain of what the question is asking before you answer. Try restating a question if you don't understand it the way it is written.

Examples

Directions: Read each item. Choose the word that means the same or about the same as the underlined word.

A resent a remark	**B** Rapid means —
A make	F foamy
B dislike	G weird
C appreciate	H short
D accept	J quick

Be careful. The letters for the answer choices change for each question. Make sure the space you fill in matches the answer you think is correct.

Practice

1 expect a package

A ship
B lose
C replace
D anticipate

2 fond recollection

F attitude
G memory
H friend
J accomplishment

3 barren area

A empty
B hot
C large
D distant

4 delightful trip

F boring
G annoying
H pleasant
J expensive

5 To intend is to —

A resist
B plan
C pay
D dislike

6 An awkward person is —

F smart
G cranky
H skilled
J clumsy

7 To revolve is to —

A jump
B fly
C fall
D turn

8 To graze is to —

F eat
G run
H stand
J sit

STOP

Examples

Directions: Read each item. Choose the answer that means the same or about the same as the underlined word.

A Load a barge	**B What is this car's maximum speed?**
A car	**Maximum means —**
B boat	F average
C plane	G normal
D cart	H lowest
	J highest

If you are not sure which answer is correct, take your best guess.

Practice

1 Jewelry made of coral

A a diamond
B a light plastic
C a hard sea deposit
D a type of glass

2 Adapt to conditions

F adjust
G accept
H agree
J allow

3 A large portion

A package
B serving
C table
D chair

4 Vivid dream

F frightening
G graphic
H long
J short

5 It was a crisp fall day.

Crisp means —

A brisk
B warm
C muggy
D windy

6 The beautiful schooner moved quickly.

A schooner is —

F an airplane
G a balloon
H a racing car
J a sailing ship

7 Lisa received an urgent message.

Urgent means —

A sad
B pressing
C exciting
D confusing

STOP

Examples

Directions: Read each item. Choose the answer that means the opposite of the underlined word.

A limp flowers	**B** an obvious solution
A stiff	**F** recent
B uncut	**G** clear
C beautiful	**H** new
D sagging	**J** hidden

 If a question is too difficult, skip it and come back to it later, if you have time.

Practice

1 the enormous bug

   A dangerous
   B harmless
   C huge
   D tiny

2 liberate people

   F imprison
   G scare
   H warn
   J free

3 considerate friend

   A attentive
   B new
   C impatient
   D thoughtless

4 the initial idea

   F worst
   G best
   H last
   J first

5 casual party

   A formal
   B easy
   C comfortable
   D exciting

6 sensible idea

   F intelligent
   G wonderful
   H common
   J foolish

7 cruel comments

   A harsh
   B kind
   C amazing
   D cautious

8 skillful performance

   F fine
   G talented
   H clumsy
   J angry

STOP

Examples   Directions: Read each item. Choose the answer you think is correct.

A | **The baby has dark brown curls.** |

In which sentence does the word **curls** mean the same thing as in the sentence above?

A English ivy curls around the window.

B The power cord lay in curls everywhere.

C The newspaper curls up in wet weather.

D After her haircut, curls covered the floor.

B   Where should I _____ this letter?

Use a _____ to smooth the edge.

F file
G place
H plane
J keep

 Read the question carefully. Use the meaning of the sentences to find the right answer.

Practice

1 | **Irene decided to wash the car.** |

In which sentence does the word **wash** mean the same thing as in the sentence above?

A We separated the wash into three piles.

B The river might wash out the dam.

C The storm flooded the dry wash.

D No one wanted to wash the dishes.

2 | **The last step is to check for errors.** |

In which sentence does the word **step** mean the same thing as in the sentence above?

F Please step over here, next to the door.

G She followed every step in the directions.

H The top step was covered with ice.

J "Step this way!" the guide told us.

3   My cousins live on this _____ .

Don't _____ the aisle near the door.

A street
B sit in
C block
D walk in

4   The _____ has a strong arm.

That _____ is for orange juice.

F player
G pitcher
H bottle
J team

5   What _____ does Carl work?

Help me _____ the box to that side.

A shift
B time
C move
D job

STOP

Spectrum Vocabulary Grade 5

Examples

Directions: Read the paragraph. Find the word below the paragraph that fits best in each numbered blank.

> Walking is one of the most ____**(A)**____ activities you can do. A brisk walk strengthens your legs, heart, and circulatory system. It's also a good way to relax and ____**(B)**____ your attitude.

A **A** exercising
    B fearsome
    C sincere
    D beneficial

B **F** rest
    G assert
    H improve
    J insist

Look for the answer that makes the most sense with the other words in the passage.

Practice

> Keeping a house warm in winter and cool in summer is a ____**(1)**____ expense for a family. There are a few ____**(2)**____ things you can do, however, that will save a great deal of money. Keep your doors closed except when they are being used. ____**(3)**____ small openings around windows and doors with caulk. Use at least twelve inches of insulation in your ____**(4)**____ or crawlspace. These three suggestions can ____**(5)**____ your ____**(6)**____ energy bill by as much as twenty percent.

1 **A** small
    B cost
    C major
    D reasonable

4 **F** room
    G attic
    H outside
    J hall

2 **F** more
    G simple
    H difficult
    J insistent

5 **A** reduce
    B increase
    C average
    D relax

3 **A** Build
    B Crack
    C Find
    D Seal

6 **F** rare
    G occasional
    H typical
    J frequent

STOP

Examples Directions: Read each question. Fill in the circle for the answer you think is correct.

A Which of these words probably comes from the Latin word *finire* meaning *to end*?

   A finer
   B finger
   C fire
   D finish

B Once we were safely inside, I heard Jorge _____ the door.

Which of these words would indicate that Jorge locked the door?

   F bolt
   G close
   H slam
   J fix

 Read each question carefully. Be sure you understand what you are supposed to do before choosing your answer.

Practice

1 Which of these words probably comes from the Latin word *collum* meaning *neck*?

   A collect
   B college
   C collar
   D calm

2 Which of these words probably comes from the Old English word *cwacian* meaning *to shake*?

   F quick
   G quake
   H creek
   J chew

---

3 The field trip was _____ to thirty students.

Which of these words means the number of students was restricted?

   A limited
   B cancelled
   C sampled
   D remarked

4 The butterfly _____ from the cocoon.

Which of these words would indicate that the butterfly came out of the cocoon?

   F reflected
   G shaped
   H furnished
   J emerged

For numbers 5 and 6, choose the answer that best defines the underlined part.

5 <u>art</u>ist   real<u>ist</u>

   A type of
   B able to
   C person who
   D always

6 <u>inter</u>cept   <u>inter</u>national

   F opposite of
   G between
   H recently
   J government

Examples   Directions: Find the word or words that mean the same or almost the same as the underlined word.

E1 alter a suit

  A purchase
  B damage
  C inspect
  D change

E2 Which of these probably comes from the Old English word *græppian* meaning *to seize*?

  F grape
  G grasp
  H eager
  J grim

For numbers 1-8, find the word or words that mean the same or almost the same as the underlined word.

1   assemble a machine

  A put together
  B take apart
  C operate
  D repair

5   An avenue is the same as a—

  A manor
  B street
  C park
  D sign

2   lasting solution

  F temporary
  G difficult
  H permanent
  J apparent

6   Something that is essential is —

  F extra
  G important
  H special
  J warm

3   open a cabinet

  A large box
  B kitchen drawer
  C wooden door
  D storage cupboard

7   A puzzle is like a —

  A sport
  B project
  C problem
  D battle

4   an exciting period

  F length of time
  G short story
  H vacation
  J game

8   If something is flimsy it is —

  F bitter
  G weak
  H strong
  J tired

GO

9 The <u>weary</u> traveler reached her home.

Weary means —

A refreshed
B excited
C tired
D worried

10 She was thrilled to have a chance to <u>conduct</u> the orchestra.

Conduct means —

F lead
G join
H tell
J name

11 The day turned out to be <u>pleasant</u>.

Pleasant means —

A unhappy
B enjoyable
C exciting
D surprising

12 When the door opened it <u>startled</u> me.

Startled means —

F angered
G tired
H pleased
J surprised

13 The teacher was pleased with my <u>accurate</u> answer.

Accurate means —

A honest
B long
C correct
D careless

For numbers 14-19, find the word that means the opposite of the underlined word.

14 being <u>humble</u>

F quiet
G angry
H sensitive
J proud

15 <u>outskirts</u> of town

A edge
B suburbs
C center
D regions

16 <u>hostile</u> people

F pleasant
G friendly
H warlike
J quiet

17 <u>irritate</u> her eyes

A soothe
B cover
C shade
D close

18 wonderful <u>triumph</u>

F victory
G experience
H contest
J loss

19 <u>successful</u> business

A profitable
B failing
C national
D local

20

For numbers 20–23, choose the word that correctly completes <u>both</u> sentences.

20 Whose _____ is it?

Be sure to _____ the water off.

F shut
G turn
H place
J position

21 The _____ crossed the bridge.

You will have to _____ hard for the race.

A bus
B prepare
C compete
D train

22 Who will keep you _____ on the trip?

Her _____ makes computers.

F entertained
G company
H business
J factory

23 We heard a great _____ last night.

A metal _____ went around the tree.

A record
B strap
C band
D concert

24 | I used a rubber <u>patch</u> to fix my bike tire. |

In which sentence does the word <u>patch</u> mean the same thing as in the sentence above?

F The rabbit ran into that big briar <u>patch</u>.

G Can they <u>patch</u> things up after the fight?

H Reg sewed a <u>patch</u> over the hole in his pants.

J A <u>patch</u> of blue appeared in the clouds.

25 | My <u>sketch</u> was better than I thought. |

In which sentence does the word <u>sketch</u> mean the same thing as in the sentence above?

A My favorite comedians did a funny <u>sketch</u> on TV last night.

B She wanted a <u>sketch</u> of her new house.

C The boy who saw the accident had to <u>sketch</u> in details for the police.

D We will <u>sketch</u> our pets in art class.

For numbers 26 and 27, choose the answer that best defines the underlined part.

26 <u>Russian</u>   <u>Hungarian</u>

F place near
G near
H person from
J well-known

27 <u>re</u>adjust   <u>re</u>capture

A like
B same as
C difficult
D again

GO

28 Which of these words probably comes from the Middle English word *facioun* meaning *manner*?

F flash
G fashion
H face
J faith

29 Which of these words probably comes from the German word *schichten* meaning *to arrange in order*?

A shift
B chief
C charge
D shelf

30 The pilot _____ the announcement about when we were going to land.

Which of these words means the pilot made the announcement again?

F landed
G argued
H repeated
J raised

31 The ingredients were _____ together.

Which of these words means the ingredients were mixed together?

A blended
B baked
C stored
D purchased

Read the paragraph. Find the word below the paragraph that fits best in each numbered blank.

Home improvement "superstores" are now ____(32)____ in large cities throughout America. These stores ____(33)____ everything for the person who wants to fix up a house or apartment, from nails to entire kitchens. To shop in one of these stores, you need at least a shopping cart, and sometimes a heavy-duty hand truck. The ____(34)____ in the superstores are specially trained to help customers find what they are looking for in these ____(35)____ hardware stores.

32 F avoided
G replaced
H exceeded
J found

33 A restrain
B prevent
C carry
D acquire

34 F personnel
G shelves
H customers
J alternatives

35 A inferior
B mammoth
C uneventful
D mere

STOP

Examples

Directions: Find the word or words that mean the same or almost the same as the underlined word.

E1 pour in a funnel

- A cup without handles
- B cone-shaped object
- C small pot
- D large pan

E2 Which of these probably comes from the Latin word *fluere* meaning *to flow*?

- F floor
- G few
- H fluent
- J flash

For numbers 1-8, find the word or words that mean the same or almost the same as the underlined word.

1 walk through the mist

- A snow
- B archway
- C fog
- D forest

2 a colorful display

- F group of birds
- G type of clothing
- H drawing
- J exhibit

3 offer expired

- A began
- B saved
- C ended
- D lasted

4 be fortunate

- F prompt
- G pleased
- H honest
- J lucky

5 A barricade is a kind of—

- A door
- B barrier
- C journey
- D statement

6 Something that is reliable is —

- F dependable
- G new
- H rich
- J unhappy

7 A forecast is like a —

- A signal
- B negative statement
- C prediction
- D positive statement

8 To mingle is to —

- F avoid
- G mix with
- H separate from
- J escape

GO

9 Do you think we can trust his opinion?

Trust means —

A understand
B believe
C hear
D summarize

10 It was a gloomy day.

Gloomy means —

F bright
G cold
H dark
J damp

11 The produce we bought at the farm stand was wonderful.

Produce means —

A canned food
B bakery products
C clothing
D fruits and vegetables

12 Victor clenched his trophy.

Clenched means —

F held tightly
G carried far
H lost
J dropped

13 We will have to delay the game.

To delay is to —

A play in spite of the weather
B put off until later
C start earlier
D play harder

For numbers 14-19, find the word that means the opposite of the underlined word.

14 an awkward puppy

F graceful
G unusual
H friendly
J clumsy

15 become weary

A happy
B stronger
C busier
D tired

16 lessen the pressure

F teach
G reduce
H increase
J forget

17 ignore a warning

A quietly whisper
B loudly shout
C listen carefully to
D pay no attention to

18 exhausted runner

F refreshed
G victorious
H frustrated
J tired

19 moist soil

A soaked
B deep
C fertile
D dry

GO

Spectrum Vocabulary Grade 5

For numbers 20–23, choose the word that correctly completes <u>both</u> sentences.

20 Randy _____ bad about the game.

We'll cover the table with _____ .

    F responded
    G felt
    H cloth
    J acted

21 The _____ of Maine is rocky.

Be careful if you _____ down the hill on your bike.

    A shore
    B speed
    C coast
    D race

22 The students _____ up for the bus.

The box is _____ with metal.

    F covered
    G stood
    H insulated
    J lined

23 Reggie wants to _____ his clothes.

All the _____ fell out of Rea's pocket.

    A change
    B money
    C pack
    D coins

24 | This test is a <u>major</u> part of your grade.

In which sentence does the word <u>major</u> mean the same thing as in the sentence above?

    F My grandfather was an Air Force <u>major</u>.
    G He plays baseball in the <u>major</u> leagues.
    H The new plant was a <u>major</u> discovery.
    J My older brother will <u>major</u> in art at the state university.

25 | The <u>number</u> seven can't be divided by two.

In which sentence does the word <u>number</u> mean the same thing as in the sentence above?

    A The winner of the drawing is <u>number</u> two-hundred ten.

    B <u>Number</u> each box, then seal it.

    C The <u>number</u> of students who came was higher than we thought.

    D A <u>number</u> of us are going to the beach.

For numbers 26 and 27, choose the answer that best defines the underlined part.

26 <u>un</u>usual   <u>un</u>kind

    F much
    G almost
    H not
    J partly

27 respect<u>able</u>   honor<u>able</u>

    A lacking a characteristic
    B possessing a characteristic
    C somewhat
    D hardly

GO ▷

28 Which of these words probably comes from the Latin word *terminare* meaning *to end*?

F torrential
G stem
H return
J terminate

29 Which of these words probably comes from the Middle English word *patron* meaning *a model*?

A pattern
B parrot
C partial
D attract

30 That gem is _____ valuable, so be sure to store it safely.

Which of these words means the gem has special value?

F particularly
G minimally
H occasionally
J repeatedly

31 The high water _____ all the way to the lower branches of the oak tree.

Which of these words means the high water reached to the lower branches of the oak tree?

A exposed
B managed
C descended
D extended

Read the paragraph. Find the word below the paragraph that fits best in each numbered blank.

The beads that ___(32)___ clothes and jewelry today have a long history. The first beads were ___(33)___ natural objects like pieces of bone, wood, or shell. Later, people learned to make beads from clay and to ___(34)___ holes in stones and pieces of metal. Beads have been used to help people count and to ___(35)___ business transactions, and in many societies, they served the same purpose as money. Some of the most extraordinary beadwork ever found was done by the native cultures in North and South America.

32 F purchase
G beneath
H support
J decorate

33 A hardly
B recently
C probably
D abruptly

34 F fill
G drill
H mine
J alert

35 A record
B cost
C cancel
D rely

Example

Directions: Read each item. Choose the answer you think is correct. Mark the space for your answer.

The desert stretched for countless miles before the travelers. It was dotted with huge dunes formed by the wind that seemed to blow forever. The six families knew the next few days were going to be the most difficult yet.	**A** **What part of a story does this passage tell about?** **A** the plot **B** the characters **C** the mood **D** the setting

 Look for key words in the question. These key words will help you understand the question and find the right answer.

Practice

1 **Which of these probably came from a newspaper article?**

A Avondo stood on the mountain peak and commanded the storm to stop.

B It was a huge rain storm that brought the family together.

C Traffic was stopped on the expressway because of flooding from the storm.

D Storms often follow the jet stream from west to east across the United States.

2 **Which of these statements from a biography expresses an opinion?**

F Ms. Lyle practices harder than most other performers.

G Her career began with a performance at Carnegie Hall.

H The audience was the largest in the history of the hall.

J Louisa's grandparents arrived in America with less than ten dollars.

3 The earthquake had thrown an unlikely group of people together, from a homeless man starting his first day on a new job to a doctor on her way to a national conference.

What part of a story does this passage tell about?

A the plot

B the characters

C the mood

D the setting

4 **Which of these statements from a magazine article expresses a fact?**

F Both candidates responded poorly to the questions from the audience.

G It is unlikely that higher taxes will benefit the people who pay them.

H Fewer than 40 percent of the people in the county voted last week.

J Voters usually support the candidate who looks best on television.

Example **Directions:** Read the passage. Find the best answer to the questions that follow the passage.

Lona arrived at the theatre early, hoping she could get a good seat. She was surprised to see that lots of other people had the same idea. The line was four blocks long! She sighed and took her place at the end of the line. Then, after a twenty minute wait, the manager came out of the theatre and announced that the show was sold out.	**A Lona discovered that the —** **A** manager was angry. **B** movie probably wasn't very good. **C** whole school had the same idea. **D** ticket line was awfully long.

Look for key words in the question, then find the same words in the passage. This will help you locate the correct answer.

Practice

Here is a passage about a birthday surprise that most young people would enjoy. Read the passage and then do numbers 1 through 7 on page 121.

"Can't you tell me yet what the surprise is?"

"No, we can't. Just relax and enjoy the scenery. We'll be there soon enough. With all your talking, I can't concentrate on my driving."

"Your mother is right. It won't be a surprise if we tell you. Trust me; you'll think it is wonderful."

Edward looked at his sister Lee Ann and shrugged his shoulders. They weren't going to tell him about the surprise. Even whining didn't work. He was so excited he felt he could explode, but there was nothing he could do about it.

In about fifteen minutes, the car pulled into a large field. Some people in the field were unloading a huge basket from a truck. Edward wondered if this was part of the surprise.

The family got out of the car and walked over to the people by the basket. Edward still didn't know what was going on. Then he saw the huge, colorful cloth on the ground. His birthday surprise was a ride in a hot air balloon!

Edward watched the crew turn the basket on its side and attach it to the balloon. They then turned on a powerful burner that forced hot air into the balloon. The hot air slowly filled the balloon and it began to rise above the basket. After about fifteen minutes, the balloon was floating above them and it had brought the basket right-side up.

"Okay, folks. We're ready. Just climb in and we'll take off."

Edward went in first. After all, it was his birthday. His father helped his mother and sister into the basket and then climbed in himself. The pilot shouted "Weight Off" and threw some sandbags to the ground. The crew let go of the lines and the balloon floated into the sky.

GO

1 **How did Edward feel during the car ride?**

   A Angry

   B Excited

   C Eager

   D Puzzled

2 **During the balloon ride, the family will be in a —**

   F basket.

   G cloth bag.

   H wooden box.

   J small room.

3 **Which of these is <u>not</u> explained in the passage?**

   A How the balloon arrived

   B How the family arrived

   C How the balloon is filled

   D How the balloon is steered

4 **Who is driving the car?**

   F Edward

   G Lee Ann

   H Mother

   J Father

5 **What does the expression "Weight Off" mean?**

   A One person should climb out of the balloon.

   B The balloon has filled and the basket has turned right-side up.

   C The pilot is ready to take off.

   D It's time to light the burner.

6 **When the family arrived—**

   F the balloon was already filled with hot air and was floating above the basket.

   G some people were unloading a basket from a truck.

   H the pilot was throwing sandbags from the basket to the ground.

   J the balloon crew was preparing a surprise party.

7 **In the last paragraph, the word *lines* refers to —**

   A ropes that keep the balloon from floating away.

   B a large number of people waiting to ride in the balloon.

   C marks on paper that show you where to write something.

   D marks on the ground where the balloon is supposed to land.

GO ⟩

Cats Great and Small

The cat that purrs sweetly when you scratch its chin is a close cousin of the lions that roam the plains of Africa and other great cats. All cats belong to the Felidae family, whose members can be found in every region of the globe except Antarctica. They are skilled hunters, and even the tamest cat will fall into a crouch if a mouse or other small animal is nearby.

Scientists believe that small, wild cats were captured and kept as pets by people as long as 10,000 years ago. The Egyptians were the first to breed cats and, for a time, cats were thought by Egyptians to be holy. As civilization spread from the Middle East to other parts of the world, cats followed. Today, cats are the most popular pet in both America and Western Europe. They are less popular in other parts of the world, and are often thought of as being pests.

The body temperature of a cat is about 101°, which is a few degrees warmer than humans. Cats are very sensitive to the temperature around them, and as the temperature rises above 95°, they pant to keep cool.

Cats have keen eyesight and have developed the ability to see well in the dark. They also have a good sense of hearing and can hear sounds beyond the range of humans. Unlike dogs, a cat's sense of smell is not particularly good.

Anyone who is familiar with both cats and dogs knows that dogs are more easily trained and seem to be more loyal. These differences can be traced to the origins of both animals. The wild ancestors of dogs were pack animals in which loyalty to the group and cooperative behavior were important for survival. The ancestors of cats were more solitary and independent, so the domestic cats of today seem less affectionate than dogs.

Another important difference between cats and dogs is that there are fewer breeds of cats. In addition, the differences among breeds are smaller than among breeds of dogs. For example, a small breed of dog may be one tenth the size of a large breed and may have much different features. Cats are all about the same size and their ears, coats, tails, and other features are very similar.

GO

8 Where would a passage like this be most likely to appear?

F In an almanac

G In a dictionary

H In a book about history

J In an encyclopedia

9 What does it mean to say that a cat will "fall into a crouch"?

A It is tired.

B It is ready to hunt.

C It is ready to purr.

D It is afraid.

10 How did cats get from the Middle East to Europe?

F They followed people as they moved or they were brought by people.

G They were there before the people moved from the Middle East.

H The Egyptians bred them.

J Cats originated in Europe.

11 What happens to cats if the temperature gets too high?

A They sweat just like people.

B Their body temperature falls.

C They begin breathing heavily.

D They become sensitive to the temperature.

12 Which part of the passage describes why cats seem less loyal than dogs?

F The ancestors of cats were more solitary and independent...

G The Egyptians were the first to breed cats...

H Unlike dogs, a cat's sense of smell is not particularly good.

J Cats are very sensitive to the temperature around them.

13 In the fifth paragraph, what does the phrase "pack animals" mean?

A Animals that stay in groups

B Good hunters

C Animals that carry things

D Animals that hunt by themselves

14 When compared with dogs, cats have —

F poor vision.

G good vision.

H a poor sense of smell.

J a keen sense of smell.

15 Who belongs to the Felidae family?

A Only domestic cats

B All cats

C Only wild cats

D All cats and dogs

STOP

Example   **Directions:** Read each passage. Find the best answer to the
questions that follow the passage.

Joe started down the ladder. He had just finished painting the window frame and he wanted to see if he had missed any spots. As he was about to step off the ladder, his knee bumped it slightly. It was just enough to send the can of paint spinning through the air. In seconds, paint was everywhere, on the ceiling, the walls, and the floor.	**A As the can fell, Joe probably felt —**
	
	  A powerless.
	
	  B proud of his work.
	
	  C pleased.
	
	  D like he had won something.

**Skim the passage then read the questions. Refer back to the
passage to find the answers to the questions.**

Practice

**Here is a passage about someone whose characters are very famous. Read the passage and then do
numbers 1 through 7 on page 125.**

Almost no young people today know who the cartoon character Oswald the
Rabbit was, but they certainly recognize his successor, Bugs Bunny. Oswald,
Bugs, and hundreds of other characters were created by Walt Disney, perhaps
the most famous cartoonist in history.

Born in Chicago in 1901, Walt Disney always wanted to be an artist. After
returning from World War I, in which he drove an ambulance, Disney worked
as a commercial artist. He enjoyed drawing cartoons more than anything else,
and decided to try his hand at a technology that was new at the time, moving
pictures.

In the 1920's, he produced several films where he made cartoon characters
move as if by magic. The technique Disney used was painstaking. He made
hundreds or even thousands of repeated drawings of the same character. In
each drawing, the character was changed just a bit. A film was taken of the
series of drawings, and when it was shown, the characters appeared to move.
The process, called animation, is still used today, although computers have
made the process much easier.

In 1928, Disney created his most famous character, Mortimer Mouse, who
we know today as Mickey. The mouse starred in a cartoon called *Steamboat
Willie*, which was unusual because it involved the use of a sound track. Within
the next few years, Disney invented many of his other characters.

The list of Disney's animation successes is long and memorable. It includes
Pinocchio, Dumbo, Bambi, Cinderella, and *Peter Pan*. Perhaps his most
remarkable animated film was *Snow White and the Seven Dwarfs*. Created in
1937, it was an immediate success. Today, more than fifty years later, it is still
one of the most popular films for children.

GO

1   What is one of the chief differences between animation today and in Walt Disney's early years?

   A   More people like animated movies.

   B   Fewer people like animated movies.

   C   Computers have made the job easier.

   D   Computers have made the job harder.

2   Which of these words best describes Walt Disney?

   F   Creative

   G   Athletic

   H   Exciting

   J   Quiet

3   What makes the film *Snow White* so remarkable?

   A   It was a great success.

   B   It took more than a year to make.

   C   It was made at a time when there were no computers.

   D   It has remained popular for more than fifty years.

4   The author of this passage would probably agree that —

   F   Oswald Rabbit is well-known today.

   G   Walt Disney was a remarkable person.

   H   animation is an easy technique.

   J   cartoons move by magic.

5   In the third paragraph, what is the meaning of the word "painstaking"?

   A   Something that hurts because it involves hard work

   B   Something that takes a long time and involves much hard work

   C   Requiring a lot of effort, like running a marathon

   D   Requiring many fine tools, such as pens and pencils

6   The secret of animation is to —

   F   make drawings that are exactly alike, then film them.

   G   choose names for characters that make people remember them.

   H   combine music, voices, and sound effects with pictures.

   J   make a film of many drawings that change just a little.

7   Which of these descriptions of the passage best supports your answer for number 6?

   A   The passage describes how Walt Disney became a cartoonist.

   B   The passage explains in detail how animation is done.

   C   The passage describes some of Walt Disney's most famous characters.

   D   The passage talks about the use of computers for animation.

GO ⟩

How did we get our alphabet?

The first writing that humans did was picture drawing. Primitive humans drew pictures of animals, hunts, storms, and other things that were important to them. These pictures have been found all around the world.

The Egyptians were probably the first people who recorded events in an organized manner. More than 5,000 years ago they started using hieroglyphics, which means "sacred writings." A hieroglyphic is a picture or symbol of a person, thing, or event. As new words were invented, more pictures were needed. The Egyptians' language grew larger and larger, so finding pictures for all the words became difficult.

The Phoenicians had a different idea. About 3,000 years ago, the Phoenicians were great sailors and traders. They traveled to many places and needed a way to keep track of their business transactions. They were the first to use symbols to represent sounds. The first letter of the Phoenician alphabet was called *aleph*. The second letter was *beth*. They were similar to our letters A and B, so in a sense, the Phoenicians even gave us the word alphabet!

The Greeks adopted the Phoenician alphabet and changed it to fit their language. They added the vowels. Later, the Romans took the Greek alphabet and changed it again to suit their language, which was Latin. Our alphabet is close to the Latin alphabet. The letter J was the last addition to the alphabet we use now; it came in the fifteenth century. Our alphabet has not changed in 500 years.

Here is an interesting alphabet story. The Egyptian civilization that developed the first picture writings died out, but their hieroglyphics carved on rocks and written on papyrus remained. No one knew what the hieroglyphics meant until 1799, when a soldier found a stone that explained their "codes." It was found near the Egyptian village of Rosetta and was called the Rosetta Stone. The stone contained Egyptian picture writing and Greek words side by side, and it said that the two were the same. This helped people figure out what the Egyptian pictures meant exactly.

K 9 ٦

A B C

GO

8 According to the article, who invented a way to represent sounds?

  F The Latins

  G The Phoenicians

  H The Greeks

  J The Romans

9 At first, writing was mostly about —

  A symbols for sounds.

  B vowels and consonants.

  C important things.

  D ancient civilizations.

10 The Phoenicians needed writing because they were —

  F warriors.

  G well educated people.

  H inventors of the Rosetta Stone.

  J sailors and traders.

11 If you wanted to figure out a message in code, it would be helpful to have something like the —

  A Rosetta Stone.

  B Egyptian hieroglyphics.

  C vowels added by the Greeks.

  D modern alphabet.

12 A great advantage of an alphabet over picture writing is that —

  F pictures must be drawn or written.

  G an alphabet can begin and end with any letter you want.

  H letters and words can be used to describe many things.

  J an alphabet can be written, but a picture must be carved in stone.

13 The passage gives you enough evidence to believe that —

  A people often adopt previous inventions and change them to suit their needs.

  B if someone had not invented writing, there could be no business today.

  C the Egyptians were the smartest people because they invented picture writing.

  D no one could have invented writing until paper was invented first.

14 The boxes below show some events described in the article.

Egyptians used hieroglyphics	Phoenicians used symbols for sounds	
1	2	3

Which of these belongs in Box 3?

  F The Phoenicians were traders.

  G The Rosetta Stone was discovered.

  H The Egyptians invented papyrus.

  J The Egyptians invented Latin.

GO

Helios and Phaethon

The people who lived in Greece long ago had good lives, but they didn't know many things that people know today. They wondered about the sun, the moon, the stars, the seasons, and all sorts of things. The Greeks made up stories to explain some of these things. Gods and goddesses were characters in these stories, and they could do magical deeds. Many people believed in the gods and goddesses then, but few people do today. Even so, the Greek stories, or myths, are still interesting to read and tell.

One Greek myth is about the sun god Helios. His job was to control the powerful horses that pulled the sun across the sky every day. They would start out in the east and pull the big, fiery ball across the heavens and drop down to earth in the west. The horses were so big and strong that the only one able to drive them was Helios.

Helios had a young son, Phaethon, who wanted to drive the sun chariot. "Please, Father, let me drive," he begged every day. "I've been helping around the stables. I can drive those horses around. I'm big enough."

One day Helios finally agreed. He went out and harnessed the horses to the sun chariot. "Drive carefully, Son," he said. Helios watched them leave.

The horses knew the way because they made the journey every day. On this day, something seemed different to them. Phaethon wasn't handling the reins the same as usual. The horses went too fast, and the boy pulled wildly on the reins and yelled. Then the horses went too low. They let the sun get so close to earth that it became burned in places. In other spots the sun chariot was so far away that the earth became icy cold.

The young Phaethon finally made it home. He was very glad to give the job of driving the horses back to his father. "I am sorry, Father. I wasn't strong enough to do your job."

The Greeks used the story of Phaethon to explain deserts and the polar regions. They believed that the places where the sun got too close and burned the earth became the deserts. When the sun was too far away, the cold areas became the North and South Poles. The Greeks used many myths to explain the facts of nature.

GO

15 Helios probably let Phaethon drive the sun chariot because —

    A Helios wanted a day off from his job.

    B Helios' wife urged him to do it.

    C Phaethon had done it before.

    D the boy begged, and Helios loved him.

16 There is enough information in the story to show that —

    F the ancient Greeks were foolish people.

    G the Greeks used myths to explain what they did not understand.

    H the Greek story was true, and we are wrong today.

    J the sun was both closer to the earth and farther away many years ago.

17 Look at the web of this story.

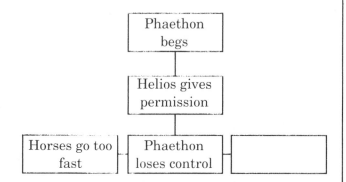

Which of these would best fit in the blank part?

    A Helios sorry, Helios punished

    B Chariot crashes into desert

    C Sun burns and freezes earth

    D Phaethon handles reins wrong

18 Which words at the end of the story show that Phaethon realized his mistake?

    F "Please, Father, let me drive."

    G "I wasn't strong enough to do your job."

    H One day Helios finally agreed.

    J Phaethon wasn't handling the reins the same as usual.

19 The author included the first paragraph in order to —

    A tell about the origin of this myth.

    B explain that the Greeks were not scientific.

    C persuade people to believe the Greek myths.

    D explain why we have seasons.

20 In order to answer number 19, the best thing to do is —

    F re-read the first paragraph.

    G skim the beginning of each paragraph.

    H make an outline of the story.

    J look for the key word "author."

21 What is another good title for this story?

    A "A Wonderful Adventure"

    B "The Sun and the Sky"

    C "How the Ground Was Burned"

    D "A Foolish Mistake"

STOP

Example   Directions: Read each passage. Find the best answer to the questions that follow the passage.

E1	To the puppy, it seemed as if —
The puppy looked at the huge mountain. He started climbing, always keeping his eyes on the little girl at the top. Finally he reached her. She bent over the little puppy and picked him up. She said, "Good job, Markey." The little puppy had just climbed a hill about four feet high.	**A** the mountain was covered with snow. **B** he was climbing a huge mountain. **C** he was a big dog at last. **D** the little girl was lost.

Here is a story about a girl who had an unusual experience. Read the story and then do numbers 1 through 6 on page 131.

Dragons aren't real, right? You read about them in fairy tales and see them in the movies, but they don't really exist. Well, I had an experience that changed my mind, and it might change your mind, too.

One night I was having trouble getting to sleep. I tossed and turned and bunched up my pillow, but nothing seemed to help. I was beginning to become drowsy when I heard a strange noise in the backyard. I got out of bed and looked out my window. There in the backyard was a huge dragon looking right at me! I rubbed my eyes, shook my head, and looked again. He was still there, and he was talking to me.

"Hey, Donna. I need your help. Something's happened and I can't fly."

This was too weird. A dragon in my backyard was talking to me, asking me to help him. My parents always told me not to talk to strange people, but not to strange dragons.

"Are you for real?" I asked.

"Of course I'm real," he answered. "Can't you see me standing in front of you? I'm as real as the nose on your face. Now, will you help me or not? I'm desperate. It's late and I want to go home."

"Sure. I'll help. What can I do?"

I decided that the easiest thing to do was to go with the flow. If this talking dragon was asking me to help him out, I might as well give it a try.

"Great. Just climb down that tree and jump on my back. You can look at my wings and see what's wrong."

"Just a second while I get changed."

"Okay, but please hurry. Sunrise is just a few hours away, and I don't want to end up in a circus."

I changed quickly and crawled out the window onto a huge tree limb. It took me only a minute to climb down to the ground. This wasn't the first time I'd taken the express route to the backyard.

"If you will just climb up my tail and take a look at my wings, you can tell me what's wrong with them. They've been bothering me for more than a week now."

"Hmm. I can see what the problem is. You don't seem to have any wings."

"Of course I do," said the dragon. "I've had them for years."

"Let me look closer."

I crawled up the dragon's tail and looked carefully at its back. I still couldn't see any wings. The only thing I could see was a pair of flaps. I stuck my hand into the flaps and felt something that could have been folded wings.

"Are your wings folded up inside your flaps?"

"My wings are inside my flaps? That must be the problem. My wings are stuck inside my flaps. What on earth will I do?"

1 **What is the "express route to the backyard?"**

A Climbing down a fire escape

B Running down the back stairs

C Running down the front stairs

D Climbing down a tree

2 **Why is the dragon worried about the sunrise?**

F He might be captured.

G It will weaken him

H He won't be able to fly.

J The sun will damage his wings.

3 **Which of these is the most likely ending for the story?**

A The dragon will fly away before sunrise.

B Donna will wake up from a dream.

C Donna will introduce the dragon to her friends.

D The dragon will end up in a circus.

4 **Why is the dragon having trouble flying?**

F The sun has affected his wings.

G He can't see in the dark.

H His wings are stuck in his flaps.

J His tail is wrapped around his wings.

5 **What does the expression "go with the flow" mean in this story?**

A To climb down the tree

B To go along with what is happening

C To go with the dragon

D To go along with a practical joke

6 **This story would be considered —**

F biography.

G non-fiction.

H fantasy.

J science.

GO ▷

Reina hated walking home from school. Even though it was just a few blocks, it was disgusting. Trash was everywhere, graffiti was all over the walls, and junked cars lined the streets. She couldn't understand how people could live that way. It was wonderful when she got home to her neat house and yard that stood out like a picture on a dingy wall.

"Mom, was our neighborhood always so terrible?"

"Not at all, Honey. Why ten years ago, this was one of the most wonderful neighborhoods in the city. People took care of their houses and had beautiful gardens. It was so nice that people came from all over to walk through the neighborhood and look at the houses." Mrs. Chavez sighed and looked away.

"I wish it were like that now. I hate being outside. It's such a mess, it makes me feel dirty."

Mrs. Chavez thought about what Reina had said. That night, after Reina was asleep, she and her husband talked it over. They decided Reina was right, and that since the city wasn't going to do anything about the neighborhood, they would have to.

On Saturday morning, Mr. Chavez knocked on his neighbor's door. He explained his idea to Mr. Jackson, who, despite being over seventy years old, agreed to help. The Chavez family and Mr. Jackson spent the morning cleaning up the trash in the tiny "pocket park" on the corner.

About noon, some of the other neighbors came out to lend a hand, even though no one had asked them. Before they knew it, there were more than twenty people working in the park. There were so many, in fact, that some of them decided to pick up the trash on the sidewalks and in the street.

Mrs. Alioto, who lived adjacent to the park, called her son and asked him to come and pick up the trash in his truck. By Saturday afternoon, the park was spotless, and the truckload of trash they had picked up was on its way to a city landfill.

For the next few weeks, the neighbors came out each evening and tackled another job. They planted flowers, continued to pick up the trash that thoughtless people kept throwing on the ground, and convinced the city to tow the junked cars away. Little by little, the neighborhood started to look better.

Reina noticed that something else was happening, too. Some of the unpleasant people who had been hanging out on her street weren't around as much. The children in the neighborhood were also playing outside more. And she didn't mind the walk home from school at all.

GO

7 **Why does Mrs. Chavez sigh and look away when Reina asks her about the neighborhood?**

A She is ignoring Reina.

B She is thinking about work.

C She is thinking about another neighborhood.

D She is remembering how it used to be.

8 **Which problem will the neighbors find most difficult to solve?**

F Finding a way to move the trash they pick up to the landfill

G Convincing thoughtless people to stop throwing trash on the ground

H Getting started

J Planting flowers

9 **In the beginning of the story, how does Reina feel about her neighborhood?**

A Happy

B Excited

C Determined

D Disgusted

10 **The reaction of the other neighbors to seeing the park cleaned up shows that**

F they wanted to help solve the problem.

G they didn't think there was much of a problem to solve.

H they enjoyed sleeping late.

J they wanted to clean up their own yards first.

11 **In the eighth paragraph, what do the words "adjacent to" mean?**

A Next to

B Far from

C Across the street from

D On the next block

12 **Why does the writer mention Mr. Jackson's age?**

F Because it is unusual for a person to be that old

G Because he was Reina's grandfather

H Because he lived adjacent to the park

J To show that older people are willing to help clean up the neighborhood

13 **What is a "pocket park"?**

A A park on a corner

B A small park

C A large park

D A park with small flowers

14 **What is the main point of this story?**

F Young people are more likely to solve problems than old people.

G Parents should listen to their children more often.

H People sometimes have to take action to solve neighborhood problems.

J Trash is a major problem in many city neighborhoods.

GO >

A Wise Warrior

Sequoya was a Cherokee Indian warrior who did a great service for his people. Sequoya saw that white settlers could read and write. He realized that the soldiers who got letters from home could read the squiggles and understand a message from someone far away. Reading and writing allowed information to be sent long distances and saved for the future.

The warrior knew that his own people had no way of recording things that were important. They could only tell the old stories and hope that their children listened and learned so that they could retell the stories to the next generation. If the Cherokees had a system of writing, Sequoya reasoned, people who had not yet been born could learn the old stories.

Sequoya called the soldiers' and settlers' books and papers "talking leaves." He thought the pages of paper looked like leaves. Sequoya decided to invent a system of writing for the Cherokees. It was not an easy task. He had to record symbols with charcoal on pieces of bark for each sound in the Cherokee language. Then he had to combine and reorganize these symbols into an alphabet. He had to come up with a simple system which would be easy for the people to learn to read and write. It took Sequoya many years to invent this alphabet.

When he finally took his alphabet to the tribal council, he had to convince them that it was usable. As a test, Sequoya left the room. The leaders were to tell his daughter something to write. She wrote it down, and he had to come back into the room and read the message. He was afraid that some problem would come up because the council asked her to write on paper with a quill pen. Before, she had always written on bark with a piece of charcoal. The council waited for him to read the message. He read, "The Cherokee nation shall live for all time." The council was convinced, and the group approved his plan.

Many Cherokees learned to read and write, and later, they published their own newspaper. Sequoya was a hero. All his time and effort had paid off. He was a warrior, but not in a war; by being wise, he had won the battle against ignorance.

GO

15 **Sequoya spent many years writing on pieces of bark with charcoal because —**

   A he was trying to learn to read English.

   B he was trying to make up an alphabet.

   C he did not like to work or hunt.

   D he did not know how to tell stories.

16 **Where did Sequoya take the alphabet for approval?**

   F To the Cherokee tribal council

   G To his family

   H To the soldiers and settlers

   J To the teachers in the school

17 **Before Sequoya's invention, the Cherokee Indians —**

   A wrote on bark with charcoal.

   B kept their history by word of mouth.

   C read the squiggles on paper.

   D didn't allow the use of writing.

18 **Sequoya first learned about writing from the —**

   F tribal elders.

   G other tribes.

   H older Cherokees who told stories.

   J soldiers and settlers.

19 **In this article, the phrase, "the next generation" means —**

   A the children's children.

   B other Indian tribes.

   C the soldiers and settlers.

   D people who can't read.

20 **There is enough information in the story to show that —**

   F writing is the only way to send information from one generation to another.

   G Sequoya learned to write at a college in the East.

   H not every group of people invented writing on their own.

   J English is the easiest language to use for writing the Cherokee language.

21 **The article is most like —**

   A a biography.

   B a folktale.

   C a story from history.

   D an adventure story.

GO

LET'S CLEAN UP OUR TOWN!

The city and the environmental council are sponsoring a clean-up campaign in all neighborhoods on Saturday, October 14. Families, clubs, organizations, and individuals are invited to participate.

Prizes will be awarded in the following categories:

- **Most trash collected (bags will be weighed)**
- **Most unusual thing picked up (judges will decide)**
- **Most people participating in a group**
- **Largest area covered**

Participants must meet at the parking lot on the corner of Pickett and St. John Streets at 8:30 AM Saturday, October 14, to register. Everyone will get an orange vest, a name tag, and trash bags. There is no limit to the ages of participants. Weigh-in and judging will take place at the same location at 3:00 PM.

PRIZES

- **free movie tickets for everyone in the group**
- **food coupons from Happy Harry's Hamburger Heaven**
- **gift certificates from Ye Olde Toy Store**
- **trophies**
- **ribbons for second and third places**

All clean-up participants are invited to a cook-out and awards presentation ceremony at Pickett and St. John at 6:00 PM.

Come out and clean up!

GO

22 Who is donating coupons as a prize?

    F Ye Olde Toy Store

    G Our Town Cinema movie theater

    H Food Basket grocery store

    J Happy Harry's Hamburger Heaven

23 Which words in the passage tell that others besides groups can participate in the clean-up?

    A ...no limit to the ages...

    B ...individuals are invited...

    C ...come out and clean up...

    D ...families, clubs, and organizations...

24 When will the prizes be awarded?

    F 6:00 PM

    G 8:30 AM

    H 3:00 PM

    J 12:00 noon

25 This announcement would probably be found in all of these places *except* —

    A the window of Happy Harry's Hamburger Heaven.

    B a local newspaper.

    C an environmental club's newsletter.

    D the Yellow Pages.

26 People who will take part in this campaign probably live in —

    F this city.

    G in the country or far suburbs.

    H in the next state.

    J in another town the same size.

27 This announcement gives you a reason to believe that —

    A the city is going to make people who litter pay fines.

    B someone will make lots of money by picking up trash on October 14.

    C the town has a problem with trash on the streets.

    D no one in this town cares enough to join in a clean-up project.

28 What other project is similar to cleaning up the town?

    F Raising money for a vacation.

    G Building a nicer house for the mayor.

    H Painting over graffiti.

    J Going to a big sale at the mall.

GO

For numbers 29 through 32, choose the best answer to the question.

29 Which of these statements from a book review expresses a fact?

A Anne Price is my favorite author, and I know many others enjoy her work.

B *The Year of the Raisin* was written by Anne Price, a native of Egypt.

C It's not the best book I ever read, but *The Year of the Raisin* is clearly on my top-ten list.

D The only real problem with *The Year of the Raisin* is that the author spends too little time describing the scenery.

30 Which of these probably came from a science fiction story?

F Scientists are still not sure how the moon was formed.

G When I was young, I was fascinated by the moon, but I never expected that some day I would help to build rockets that would fly there.

H NASA reported today that the next space shot would be delayed at least one day because of the weather.

J The vessel approached the domed city that had been established on the dark side of the moon.

31 Which of these statements from a newspaper article expresses an opinion?

A The principal language in England is, of course, English, but it is spoken differently from American English.

B London is served by an extensive subway system called the Underground that circles the city.

C Automobiles in England have the steering wheel on the right, which is the opposite of American cars.

D A trip to England is inexpensive, and people generally have a good time, even when the weather is poor.

32 Most of the people in Folsom were what most of us think of as being normal. The Rayburn's, however, were not. From the house in which they lived to their hobbies, they were most unusual.

Which part of a story does this passage tell about?

F The setting

G The characters

H The plot

J The mood

STOP

Example   Directions: Read the selection, then choose the best answer to the question.

E1

Officers of the First Central Bank announced yesterday that construction of the West Avenue branch will begin on March 1. If all goes according to plan, the branch office will be finished by August 15. When the new branch is completed, First Central Bank will have a total of 7 offices in town, including the central office on Powell Street. The last branch office was opened on October 8 of last year.

When will the West Avenue branch of the First Central Bank be finished?

A March 1

B October 8

C August 15

D August 7

Here is a story about a remarkable historic discovery. Read the story and then do numbers 1 through 8 on page 140.

In 1879, a group of explorers made an incredible find. They discovered paintings of remarkable beauty on the walls of a cave in Spain. Some scientists believed that these paintings were created by early humans from the Stone Age, between ten and thirty thousand years ago. Other scientists and the public did not believe the claim, but over the years, it was proven correct. Our ancestors had incredible artistic talents.

Most of the cave art that has been discovered has been found in Spain and France. A smaller number of such caves are located in Italy, Portugal, Russia, and other countries. Scientists believe that many more caves will be discovered in the coming years, and are concentrating their efforts on Africa and the area between Europe and Asia. These two regions of the world were populated first by humans.

Cave art was carved or painted on the walls and roofs of caves, usually near the entrance. The entrance area was probably chosen to take advantage of daylight and to allow many people to view the paintings. In some cases, the art appears much deeper in caves and requires artificial light. Evidence suggests that the artists used torches or shallow bowls in which animal fat was burned.

Primitive artists were able to create with a wide variety of colors, including yellow, red, brown, green, and black. These colors came from minerals that were ground and mixed with animal fat, vegetable juice, water, or even blood. The colors were applied with sticks or brushes made of animal hair. One of the most unusual means of applying color was to blow it through a hollow reed.

The most popular subject of cave art was animals. They included mammoths, horses, deer, bison, cave lions, wild cattle, and wooly rhinoceros. Many of the animals shown in cave paintings are now extinct. Scientists are not sure why early humans made cave paintings, but some of the paintings appear to show successful hunts, while others might have been intended to bring good luck during upcoming hunts. Other popular subjects include human figures, battles, and surprisingly, human hands. The outlines of human hands have been found on every continent where humans created cave art.

GO

1 What was the response of the general public to the discovery of cave art made by Stone Age people?

   A They believed it at first.

   B They did not believe it.

   C They thought it was beautiful.

   D They ignored it.

2 From cave paintings, scientists learned that —

   F Stone Age people thought caves were sacred places.

   G animals were not hunted for food during the Stone Age.

   H some animals that are extinct now were alive during the Stone Age.

   J the temperature was much warmer during the Stone Age.

3 Based on the passage, what can you conclude about animal fat?

   A It does not burn.

   B Stone Age artists used it to preserve their paintings.

   C It can be burned to produce light.

   D Stone Age artists mixed it with their food.

4 Where do scientists expect to find more cave paintings?

   F In Central and South America

   G In Spain and France

   H In places where there are caves with large openings

   J In regions of the world first populated by humans

5 In the fourth paragraph, what does the word "primitive" mean?

   A European or African

   B Talented

   C Untalented

   D Early in history

6 Paintings that were created deep inside caves —

   F could be viewed easily by daylight.

   G were always made using the juice from plants.

   H were probably seen by fewer people than paintings near the entrance.

   J usually show more animals than paintings near the entrance.

7 What can you conclude about minerals?

   A Primitive humans knew how to turn minerals into metal.

   B Different types of minerals can be used to make different kinds of colors.

   C Different types of minerals were used to represent different animals.

   D The minerals used for paintings were always found in caves.

8 Where would this passage be most likely to appear?

   F In a textbook about early human history

   G In a textbook about modern art

   H In a dictionary

   J In an encyclopedia entry about caves

GO

In this story, a cowgirl finds herself lost in a sudden storm. She finds her way into a canyon that shelters her from the storm. Read the story, then do numbers 9 through 14.

Mystery Canyon

"New Year's Eve is one heck of a time to freeze to death," Rose muttered to herself. She scrunched down into her duster and tried to warm up, but it was pretty much hopeless. She wished she were back at home with the kids and Grandpa, but she had a job to do. This herd of cows was a year's worth of mortgage, and she wasn't about to lose a single head.

When she had started out that morning, it was a New Mexico blue sky day. At about noon she had caught up with her herd of beefers and was heading them back to the pasture near the house. The sky by then was leaden, and by one o'clock, the snow had started to fall. Within an hour, the storm had turned real nasty, and she couldn't see fifty yards in front of her. She had finally given up and was looking for a tree, a large rock, anything that might give them shelter from the wind and snow.

"This isn't the worst, Chico. Remember that sandstorm last summer? I had to tie my bandannas over your nose and mouth, but you still got us home with your eyes closed. I know you'll get us out of this jam."

Her voice was calm and encouraging, and Chico responded by pushing a little harder through the snow. The cows were still with them, but they were clearly tiring. Rose knew they wouldn't last much longer without a rest. She was worried, but was a long way from panic. Somebody once said about Rose that a brick would panic before she did, and they were right. She'd been through some terrible times on the range, and this was just one more thing she'd deal with.

Chico continued to trudge on, and the steers did their best to stay up with the strong, young horse. Within fifteen minutes, however, Rose knew it was hopeless to go on, and she and Chico rounded the herd into a tight group. With some luck, they might all survive the night.

Knowing how dangerous it would be to fall asleep, Rose struggled to stay awake, when the tinkling of bells jolted her back to consciousness. For a moment she thought she was imagining the sound, then it happened again. Chico and the steers must have heard it, for their ears perked up and they all turned in the same direction. As if on cue, Chico and the herd started moving toward the sound.

In a few minutes, Chico had led them to a narrow canyon. It's towering walls blocked the wind, and the small stream flowing through it seemed to warm the air slightly. Chico sniffed the air for an instant and then headed confidently into the canyon.

The canyon broadened slightly as they continued into it and a few trees showed themselves through the storm. A little farther along Rose discovered the source of the tinkling. A small cabin nestled at the end of the canyon, and on the porch, a harness hung from nails. With each gust of wind, the bells on the harness dropped a handful of notes.

Chico walked to the cabin as if it were a home he had always known. The cows moved into the pasture and started grazing on the tufts of grass that reached through the snow. Even Rose felt a tingling warmth, the same feeling she had

GO

known as a little girl when she rushed into her grandmother's kitchen after a long, cold ride home from school.

The front door of the cabin opened and a head stuck out. "Take your horse into the barn. You can unsaddle in there and give him some hay and water. Then come on in the back door. It's too awful out there for an old man to be more neighborly."

Rose took care of Chico and trudged over to the cabin. Before she stepped inside, she saw a few deer had joined her cows in the pasture. A row of mountain bluebirds lined the fence around the pasture, and in the cottonwoods by the stream sat a pair of owls who watched her every move. The yellow eyes of several coyotes sparked in the deeper parts of the canyon, but they seemed so tame that she didn't think they posed any threat to the herd.

"Quite a bunch of critters out there," Rose said as she walked through the door. "I guess this storm has made buddies of all the locals. My name's Rose, and I'm sure glad to meet you."

"I'm Sandy, or at least that's what they call me, although my hair's not been that color for a longer time than I can remember." His white hair was gathered into a ponytail that hung down the back of his flannel shirt. "The ponytail's not a fashion statement. I just don't get to the barber very often, and well, this is pretty easy to take care of. Can I get you something warm? Here, sit down by the fire."

"Anything warm would be great," sighed Rose, "and I'd love to sit down by that fire."

"You're the Shipley girl, aren't you?" Sandy asked as he handed her a cup of tea. "Your folks have been around here for quite a spell. How's the family?"

"Grandmother died a few years ago. Grandpa's living with me and the kids now. How long have you lived here? I didn't know there was a ranch or even a canyon back here."

"It's easy to miss, and I kind of like my privacy. If you ride below the ridge you can't see the opening, and not many folks have any reason to climb the ridge."

9 By the end of the passage, the feelings of the girl have changed from —

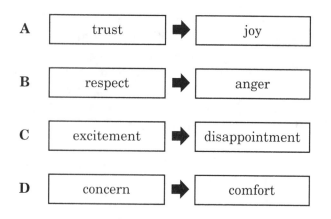

A trust ➡ joy

B respect ➡ anger

C excitement ➡ disappointment

D concern ➡ comfort

GO

10 Rose was most concerned about losing the cows because they were a "year's worth of mortgage." Which of these means about the same as a *year's worth of mortgage*?

    F Money needed for a family vacation this year

    G Money needed to pay for the house for a year

    H A long period of time without money

    J Something worth more than she would earn in a year

11 The relationship between Rose and her horse Chico is most like —

    A two friends who have worked together a long time.

    B a stranger helping out a person she just met.

    C a boy making a new student in the class feel comfortable.

    D an experienced doctor knowing what to do when someone is hurt.

12 How does the author describe the sound of the bells?

    F A noise that frightened Chico and the cows

    G Coyotes howling deep in the canyon among the trees

    H Notes being dropped

    J As loud as the wind that was howling around Rose and Chico

13 What is the most important thing the author wants you to know about the canyon?

    A The stream in the canyon kept the air warm.

    B There was a barn in the canyon that Rose could use for Chico.

    C In the canyon, animals were friendlier than they were in other places.

    D It was hidden and Rose didn't know about it.

14 Which of these ideas suggests the canyon is more special than it first appears?

    F The cows ate the grass in the canyon, even though it was snowing hard and was windy.

    G Rose and Chico felt comfortable in the canyon, even though they had never been there before.

    H Birds were sitting on the fence.

    J The walls of the canyon blocked the wind.

GO >

Here is a passage about an important part of every plant. Read the story and then do numbers 15 through 17.

The roots of trees, shrubs, and other plants perform two major functions. Roots keep the plant upright in the same place, and they feed the plant by absorbing moisture and nutrients from the soil.

Different plants have different kinds of roots. The roots of some plants go deep into the soil, while others spread out sideways for great distances. You might be surprised to learn that the giant redwoods of California have relatively shallow roots. This is because they grow in the mountains where there is very little soil. The shallow roots allow the trees to absorb as much moisture as possible. Unfortunately, a strong wind can blow a redwood tree down much more easily than other, smaller trees with deeper roots.

If you look closely at small roots, you will see that they are delicate. Don't be fooled by their appearance. Tiny roots can work their way into the smallest spaces and can crack the hardest stones. When roots have established themselves well in the soil, it is almost impossible to remove the plant without damaging it.

The roots of all plants share several common characteristics. One is geotropism, the tendency to grow down into the earth. In other words, roots follow the pull of gravity. If you plant a seed upside down and watch it grow, you will notice that the young root will emerge from the top of the seed and then turn immediately down.

A second characteristic is hydrotropism. Roots have a tendency to grow in the direction of water. If the source of water is deep in the soil, the roots will grow down. If the source of water is near the surface, the roots will grow sideways. Hydrotropism can be a problem for home owners who landscape with certain plants. Willow trees, for example, love moisture, and will send their roots in the direction of the nearest source of water. Near a house, this is often underground water or sewer pipes, which will become clogged with tree roots.

A third characteristic roots share is the ability to regenerate the plant. Under certain conditions, a tiny piece of root can be nurtured so it grows into a new plant. The process of regeneration happens sometimes in nature with hardy species like dandelions and bamboo. In the highly controlled environment of a laboratory or greenhouse, almost every plant can be regenerated from a healthy piece of root.

Roots are not usually considered to be an attractive part of a plant. In some Asian countries, however, the roots of trees may be trained to grow above ground into exotic shapes. This is especially true with bonsai plants, miniature versions of full-sized plants. The process of training the roots and the other parts of the plant is painstaking and takes many years.

15 **According to the passage, geotropism is the tendency for roots to —**

A grow downward in response to gravity.

B grow downward in response to moisture.

C grow upward in response to gravity.

D grow upward in response to moisture.

16 **Which of these would be the best title for the passage?**

F "How Roots Grow"

G "Tropism"

H "Shallow and Deep Roots"

J "Remarkable Roots"

17 **Desert plants often have large but shallow root systems. This is probably because —**

A the principal source of moisture is underground springs.

B the principal source of moisture is occasional rain.

C there is less gravity in the desert.

D there is more gravity in the desert.

GO

Finding Our Heritage

Historic Pleasanton, the city's history and heritage council, is sponsoring a contest for young people's organizations. Clubs such as Scouts, church groups, and even neighborhood groups are encouraged to participate. Prizes will be awarded in each age group. The council will provide money for eligible projects entered in the contest.

If you would like to enter, send a letter with the following information:

1. Your plan for exploring our history or heritage. Describe the purpose of the project, what you intend to do, and how you will let the public know what you found. (Newspaper article, booklet, computer program, video, etc.)
2. The cost of your project. List items that must be bought and their prices.
3. The number of people in your group.
4. The age of the people in your group.
5. The names of the adult sponsors, their addresses and their telephone numbers.
6. The date you hope to begin and the length of time this project will take.

Plans must be submitted no later than May 31. Projects must be completed by September 1.

For more information, call Julia Happyhands, 214-555-5432. Send letters to:
Historic Pleasanton
1234 Good Street
Pleasanton, Texas 75432

The adult sponsors will be notified if the group is chosen. Projects will be judged when they are completed. Winners will also be honored at the Pleasanton Fall Festival in October. Winning groups will ride on floats in the Fall Festival Parade.

GO

18 Groups who wish to enter the contest should first —

    F get the money to pay for their project.

    G start working on their project.

    H write a letter to the council.

    J call Ms. Happyhands

19 Projects that will be considered for prizes must —

    A be entered by young people's organizations.

    B investigate how the United States grew from a colony to a real country.

    C deal with solving today's problems.

    D focus on creating more jobs in the town.

20 The heritage contest announcement might be posted in all of these places *except* a —

    F local newspaper.

    G message board at Pleasanton City Hall.

    H bulletin boards at local shopping malls.

    J newspaper ad in a city 100 miles away.

21 These directions were written in order to —

    A tell how to do a good deed.

    B offer money for making Pleasanton more popular.

    C get people to ride on floats in the parade.

    D present guidelines for entering the contest.

22 Which of these groups would *not* be eligible for the contest?

    F Adults working for a business in Pleasanton

    G A Girl Scout troop of 10-year-olds

    H Three families of children aged 5 to 15

    J A summer camp class of 12-year-olds at the YMCA

23 The purpose of sending the letter to the council is to —

    A let people know what the name of your group is.

    B help the council decide on a name for the contest.

    C show that a group can actually complete a project.

    D get more information from the council.

24 Groups who are winners will receive —

    F materials for their projects.

    G prizes and honors at the Fall Festival.

    H blue ribbons for each participant.

    J a money prize of $100.

GO

For numbers 25 through 28, choose the best answer to the question.

25 **Which of these probably came from the beginning of a book about young people who solve a mystery?**

A The young people gathered in Wilson Park and waited quietly. They expected the spring to begin flowing again any minute, if all went well.

B Wilson Park was named after Jasper Wilson, a merchant who opened the first grocery in Lansdale soon after the town was founded.

C For more than 200 years, a spring had fed the pond at the edge of Wilson Park. Last year, for some unknown reason, the spring simply stopped flowing.

D As they climbed the cliff, Jennie and Roberto could hear the sound of water, but no matter how hard they looked, they couldn't see it.

26 **Which of these statements from an encyclopedia expresses a fact?**

F Mozart is recognized as being the greatest composer in history.

G Because of technology, there are more ways to enjoy music than ever before.

H The finest music was composed during the seventeenth and eighteenth centuries.

J Musicians today are less talented than those of twenty years ago.

27 The crowd at the beach was having a wonderful time. The sky was clear, the sun was bright, and the ocean temperature was almost perfect.

What part of a story does this passage tell about?

A The plot

B The characters

C The mood

D The setting

28 **Which of these statements probably came from a true story about the natural world?**

F The fall migration of sandhill cranes begins in northern Canada and ends many thousands of miles away in Texas or New Mexico.

G The hawks looked at one another, nodded their heads, and agreed the cliff would make a wonderful home for them and their chicks.

H "I'm too dull," the mallard thought. "I could use more colorful feathers."

J The geese laughed at the fox who had fallen into the pond and was very unhappy.

STOP

Grade 5 Answer Key

Page 105
A. B
B. J
1. D
2. G
3. A
4. H
5. B
6. J
7. D
8. F

Page 106
A. B
B. J
1. C
2. F
3. B
4. G
5. A
6. J
7. B

Page 107
A. A
B. J
1. D
2. F
3. D
4. H
5. A
6. J
7. B
8. H

Page 108
A. D
B. F
1. D
2. G
3. C
4. G
5. A

Page 109
A. D
B. H
1. C
2. G
3. D
4. G
5. A
6. H

Page 110
A. D
B. F
1. C
2. G
3. A
4. J
5. C
6. G

Page 111
E1. D
E2. G
1. A
2. H
3. D
4. F
5. B
6. G
7. C
8. G

Page 112
9. C
10. F
11. B
12. J
13. C
14. J
15. C
16. G

Grade 5 Answer Key

17. A
18. J
19. B

Page 113
20. G
21. D
22. G
23. C
24. H
25. B
26. H
27. D

Page 114
28. G
29. A
30. H
31. A
32. J
33. C
34. F
35. B

Page 115
E1. B
E2. H
1. C
2. J
3. C
4. J
5. B
6. F
7. C
8. G

Page 116
9. B
10. H
11. F

12. F
13. B
14. F
15. B
16. H
17. C
18. F
19. D

Page 117
20. G
21. C
22. J
23. A
24. H
25. A
26. H
27. B

Page 118
28. J
29. A
30. F
31. D
32. J
33. C
34. G
35. A

Page 119
A. D
1. C
2. F
3. B
4. H

Page 120
A. D

Grade 5 Answer Key

Page 121
1. B
2. F
3. D
4. H
5. C
6. G
7. A

Page 123
8. J
9. B
10. F
11. C
12. F
13. A
14. H
15. B

Page 124
A. A

Page 125
1. C
2. F
3. D
4. G
5. B
6. J
7. B

Page 127
8. G
9. C
10. J
11. A
12. H
13. A
14. G

Page 129
15. D
16. G
17. C
18. G
19. B
20. F
21. D

Page 130
E1. B

Page 131
1. D
2. F
3. B
4. H
5. B
6. H

Page 133
7. D
8. G
9. D
10. F
11. A
12. J
13. B
14. H

Page 135
15. B
16. F
17. B
18. J
19. A
20. H
21. C

Grade 5 Answer Key

Page 137
22. J
23. B
24. F
25. D
26. F
27. C
28. H

Page 138
29. B
30. J
31. D
32. G

Page 139
E1. C

Page 140
1. B
2. H
3. C
4. J
5. D
6. H
7. B
8. F

Page 142
9. D

Page 143
10. G
11. A
12. H
13. D
14. G

Page 144
15. A
16. J
17. B

Page 146
18. H
19. A
20. J
21. D
22. F
23. C
24. G

Page 147
25. C
26. G
27. D
28. F

Fill in only one letter for each item. If you change an answer, make sure to erase your first mark completely.

Page 105

A. (A) (B) (C) (D)

B. (F) (G) (H) (J)

1. (A) (B) (C) (D)

2. (F) (G) (H) (J)

3. (A) (B) (C) (D)

4. (F) (G) (H) (J)

5. (A) (B) (C) (D)

6. (F) (G) (H) (J)

7. (A) (B) (C) (D)

8. (F) (G) (H) (J)

Page 106

A. (A) (B) (C) (D)

B. (F) (G) (H) (J)

1. (A) (B) (C) (D)

2. (F) (G) (H) (J)

3. (A) (B) (C) (D)

4. (F) (G) (H) (J)

5. (A) (B) (C) (D)

6. (F) (G) (H) (J)

7. (A) (B) (C) (D)

Page 107

A. (A) (B) (C) (D)

B. (F) (G) (H) (J)

1. (A) (B) (C) (D)

2. (F) (G) (H) (J)

3. (A) (B) (C) (D)

4. (F) (G) (H) (J)

5. (A) (B) (C) (D)

6. (F) (G) (H) (J)

7. (A) (B) (C) (D)

8. (F) (G) (H) (J)

Page 108

A. (A) (B) (C) (D)

B. (F) (G) (H) (J)

1. (A) (B) (C) (D)

2. (F) (G) (H) (J)

3. (A) (B) (C) (D)

4. (F) (G) (H) (J)

5. (A) (B) (C) (D)

Page 109

A. (A) (B) (C) (D)

B. (F) (G) (H) (J)

1. (A) (B) (C) (D)

2. (F) (G) (H) (J)

3. (A) (B) (C) (D)

4. (F) (G) (H) (J)

5. (A) (B) (C) (D)

6. (F) (G) (H) (J)

Page 110

A. (A) (B) (C) (D)

B. (F) (G) (H) (J)

1. (A) (B) (C) (D)

2. (F) (G) (H) (J)

3. (A) (B) (C) (D)

4. (F) (G) (H) (J)

5. (A) (B) (C) (D)

6. (F) (G) (H) (J)

Page 111

E1. (A) (B) (C) (D)

E2. (F) (G) (H) (J)

1. (A) (B) (C) (D)

2. (F) (G) (H) (J)

3. (A) (B) (C) (D)

4. (F) (G) (H) (J)

5. (A) (B) (C) (D)

6. (F) (G) (H) (J)

7. (A) (B) (C) (D)

8. (F) (G) (H) (J)

Page 112

9. (A) (B) (C) (D)

10. (F) (G) (H) (J)

11. (A) (B) (C) (D)

12. (F) (G) (H) (J)

13. (A) (B) (C) (D)

14. (F) (G) (H) (J)

15. (A) (B) (C) (D)

16. (F) (G) (H) (J)

17. (A) (B) (C) (D)

18. (F) (G) (H) (J)

19. (A) (B) (C) (D)

Page 113

20. (F) (G) (H) (J)

21. (A) (B) (C) (D)

22. (F) (G) (H) (J)

23. (A) (B) (C) (D)

24. (F) (G) (H) (J)

25. (A) (B) (C) (D)

26. (F) (G) (H) (J)

27. (A) (B) (C) (D)

Page 114

28. (F) (G) (H) (J)

29. (A) (B) (C) (D)

30. (F) (G) (H) (J)

31. (A) (B) (C) (D)

32. (F) (G) (H) (J)

33. (A) (B) (C) (D)

34. (F) (G) (H) (J)

35. (A) (B) (C) (D)

Page 115

E1. (A) (B) (C) (D)

E2. (F) (G) (H) (J)

1. (A) (B) (C) (D)

2. (F) (G) (H) (J)

3. (A) (B) (C) (D)

4. (F) (G) (H) (J)

5. (A) (B) (C) (D)

6. (F) (G) (H) (J)

7. (A) (B) (C) (D)

8. (F) (G) (H) (J)

Page 116

9. (A) (B) (C) (D)

10. (F) (G) (H) (J)

11. (A) (B) (C) (D)

12. (F) (G) (H) (J)

13. (A) (B) (C) (D)

14. (F) (G) (H) (J)

15. (A) (B) (C) (D)

16. (F) (G) (H) (J)

17. (A) (B) (C) (D)

18. (F) (G) (H) (J)

19. (A) (B) (C) (D)

Page 117

20. (F) (G) (H) (J)

21. (A) (B) (C) (D)

22. (F) (G) (H) (J)

23. (A) (B) (C) (D)

24. (F) (G) (H) (J)

25. Ⓐ Ⓑ Ⓒ Ⓓ
26. Ⓕ Ⓖ Ⓗ Ⓙ
27. Ⓐ Ⓑ Ⓒ Ⓓ

Page 118

28. Ⓕ Ⓖ Ⓗ Ⓙ
29. Ⓐ Ⓑ Ⓒ Ⓓ
30. Ⓕ Ⓖ Ⓗ Ⓙ
31. Ⓐ Ⓑ Ⓒ Ⓓ
32. Ⓕ Ⓖ Ⓗ Ⓙ
33. Ⓐ Ⓑ Ⓒ Ⓓ
34. Ⓕ Ⓖ Ⓗ Ⓙ
35. Ⓐ Ⓑ Ⓒ Ⓓ

Page 119

A. Ⓐ Ⓑ Ⓒ Ⓓ
1. Ⓐ Ⓑ Ⓒ Ⓓ
2. Ⓕ Ⓖ Ⓗ Ⓙ
3. Ⓐ Ⓑ Ⓒ Ⓓ
4. Ⓕ Ⓖ Ⓗ Ⓙ

Page 120

A. Ⓐ Ⓑ Ⓒ Ⓓ

Page 121

1. Ⓐ Ⓑ Ⓒ Ⓓ
2. Ⓕ Ⓖ Ⓗ Ⓙ
3. Ⓐ Ⓑ Ⓒ Ⓓ
4. Ⓕ Ⓖ Ⓗ Ⓙ

5. Ⓐ Ⓑ Ⓒ Ⓓ
6. Ⓕ Ⓖ Ⓗ Ⓙ
7. Ⓐ Ⓑ Ⓒ Ⓓ

Page 123

8. Ⓕ Ⓖ Ⓗ Ⓙ
9. Ⓐ Ⓑ Ⓒ Ⓓ
10. Ⓕ Ⓖ Ⓗ Ⓙ
11. Ⓐ Ⓑ Ⓒ Ⓓ
12. Ⓕ Ⓖ Ⓗ Ⓙ
13. Ⓐ Ⓑ Ⓒ Ⓓ
14. Ⓕ Ⓖ Ⓗ Ⓙ
15. Ⓐ Ⓑ Ⓒ Ⓓ

Page 124

A. Ⓐ Ⓑ Ⓒ Ⓓ

Page 125

1. Ⓐ Ⓑ Ⓒ Ⓓ
2. Ⓕ Ⓖ Ⓗ Ⓙ
3. Ⓐ Ⓑ Ⓒ Ⓓ
4. Ⓕ Ⓖ Ⓗ Ⓙ
5. Ⓐ Ⓑ Ⓒ Ⓓ
6. Ⓕ Ⓖ Ⓗ Ⓙ
7. Ⓐ Ⓑ Ⓒ Ⓓ

Page 127

8. Ⓕ Ⓖ Ⓗ Ⓙ
9. Ⓐ Ⓑ Ⓒ Ⓓ
10. Ⓕ Ⓖ Ⓗ Ⓙ

11. Ⓐ Ⓑ Ⓒ Ⓓ
12. Ⓕ Ⓖ Ⓗ Ⓙ
13. Ⓐ Ⓑ Ⓒ Ⓓ
14. Ⓕ Ⓖ Ⓗ Ⓙ

Page 129

15. Ⓐ Ⓑ Ⓒ Ⓓ
16. Ⓕ Ⓖ Ⓗ Ⓙ
17. Ⓐ Ⓑ Ⓒ Ⓓ
18. Ⓕ Ⓖ Ⓗ Ⓙ
19. Ⓐ Ⓑ Ⓒ Ⓓ
20. Ⓕ Ⓖ Ⓗ Ⓙ
21. Ⓐ Ⓑ Ⓒ Ⓓ

Page 130

E1. Ⓐ Ⓑ Ⓒ Ⓓ

Page 131

1. Ⓐ Ⓑ Ⓒ Ⓓ
2. Ⓕ Ⓖ Ⓗ Ⓙ
3. Ⓐ Ⓑ Ⓒ Ⓓ
4. Ⓕ Ⓖ Ⓗ Ⓙ
5. Ⓐ Ⓑ Ⓒ Ⓓ
6. Ⓕ Ⓖ Ⓗ Ⓙ

Page 133

7. Ⓐ Ⓑ Ⓒ Ⓓ
8. Ⓕ Ⓖ Ⓗ Ⓙ
9. Ⓐ Ⓑ Ⓒ Ⓓ
10. Ⓕ Ⓖ Ⓗ Ⓙ

11. Ⓐ Ⓑ Ⓒ Ⓓ
12. Ⓕ Ⓖ Ⓗ Ⓙ
13. Ⓐ Ⓑ Ⓒ Ⓓ
14. Ⓕ Ⓖ Ⓗ Ⓙ

Page 135

15. Ⓐ Ⓑ Ⓒ Ⓓ
16. Ⓕ Ⓖ Ⓗ Ⓙ
17. Ⓐ Ⓑ Ⓒ Ⓓ
18. Ⓕ Ⓖ Ⓗ Ⓙ
19. Ⓐ Ⓑ Ⓒ Ⓓ
20. Ⓕ Ⓖ Ⓗ Ⓙ
21. Ⓐ Ⓑ Ⓒ Ⓓ

Page 137

22. Ⓕ Ⓖ Ⓗ Ⓙ
23. Ⓐ Ⓑ Ⓒ Ⓓ
24. Ⓕ Ⓖ Ⓗ Ⓙ
25. Ⓐ Ⓑ Ⓒ Ⓓ
26. Ⓕ Ⓖ Ⓗ Ⓙ
27. Ⓐ Ⓑ Ⓒ Ⓓ
28. Ⓕ Ⓖ Ⓗ Ⓙ

Page 138

29. Ⓐ Ⓑ Ⓒ Ⓓ
30. Ⓕ Ⓖ Ⓗ Ⓙ
31. Ⓐ Ⓑ Ⓒ Ⓓ
32. Ⓕ Ⓖ Ⓗ Ⓙ

Page 139

E1. Ⓐ Ⓑ Ⓒ Ⓓ

Page 140

1. Ⓐ Ⓑ Ⓒ Ⓓ
2. Ⓕ Ⓖ Ⓗ Ⓙ
3. Ⓐ Ⓑ Ⓒ Ⓓ
4. Ⓕ Ⓖ Ⓗ Ⓙ
5. Ⓐ Ⓑ Ⓒ Ⓓ
6. Ⓕ Ⓖ Ⓗ Ⓙ
7. Ⓐ Ⓑ Ⓒ Ⓓ
8. Ⓕ Ⓖ Ⓗ Ⓙ

Page 142

9. Ⓐ Ⓑ Ⓒ Ⓓ

Page 143

10. Ⓕ Ⓖ Ⓗ Ⓙ
11. Ⓐ Ⓑ Ⓒ Ⓓ
12. Ⓕ Ⓖ Ⓗ Ⓙ
13. Ⓐ Ⓑ Ⓒ Ⓓ
14. Ⓕ Ⓖ Ⓗ Ⓙ

Page 144

15. Ⓐ Ⓑ Ⓒ Ⓓ
16. Ⓕ Ⓖ Ⓗ Ⓙ
17. Ⓐ Ⓑ Ⓒ Ⓓ

Page 146

18. (F) (G) (H) (J)

19. (A) (B) (C) (D)

20. (F) (G) (H) (J)

21. (A) (B) (C) (D)

22. (F) (G) (H) (J)

23. (A) (B) (C) (D)

24. (F) (G) (H) (J)

Page 147

25. (A) (B) (C) (D)

26. (F) (G) (H) (J)

27. (A) (B) (C) (D)

28. (F) (G) (H) (J)

Notes

Notes